Marco Polo

Voyager to the Orient

by Carol Greene

Marco Polo
Voyager to the Orient

by Carol Greene

HOUGHTON MIFFLIN COMPANY BOSTON

Atlanta   Dallas   Geneva, Illinois   Palo Alto   Princeton   Toronto

PICTURE ACKNOWLEDGMENTS

Historical Pictures Service, Chicago—4, 10, 34, 47, 48, 49 (2 photos), 50 (2 photos), 51, 52 (2 photos), 53, 54, 60, 74, 84, 94
Horizon Graphics—map on pages 100-101
Cover illustration by Len W. Meents

Copyright © 1987 by Childrens Press,™ Inc.

Houghton Mifflin Edition, 1993

No part of this work may be reproduced or transmitted in any form or by any means, electronic or mechanical, including photocopying and recording, or by any information storage or retrieval system without the prior written permission of the copyright owner unless such copying is expressly permitted by federal copyright law. With the exception of non-profit transcription in Braille, Houghton Mifflin is not authorized to grant permission for further uses of this work. Permission must be obtained from the individual copyright owner as identified herein.

Printed in the U.S.A.

ISBN 0-395-61844-4

123456789-B-96 95 94 93 92

Table of Contents

Chapter 1
    Marco and the Queen of the Adriatic   11

Chapter 2
    The Missing Father   17

Chapter 3
    A Slow Beginning   23

Chapter 4
    The Long Journey   27

Chapter 5
    Pomp and Pleasures   35

Chapter 6
    The Story of the Khans   41

Chapter 7
    Life with Kublai   55

Chapter 8
    On the Road   61

Chapter 9
    The Golden Web   69

Chapter 10
     Voyage of Wonders   75

Chapter 11
     Homecoming   85

Chapter 12
     A Prison and a Book   89

Chapter 13
     The Later Years   95

Map   100

Time Line   102

Index   104

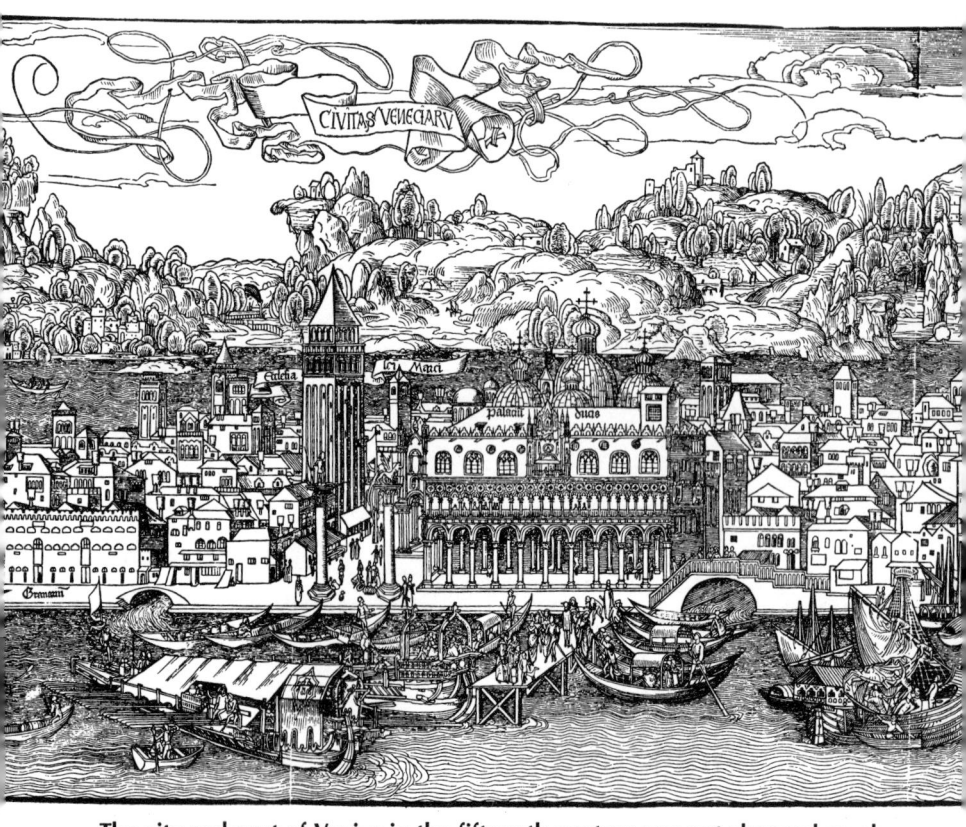

The city and port of Venice in the fifteenth century was not changed much from Marco Polo's time. As a child, Marco could spend hours at the wharves watching ships from Europe, Asia Minor, North Africa, and India.

Chapter 1

MARCO AND THE QUEEN OF THE ADRIATIC

Like an enchanted kingdom, the city-republic of Venice rose from the Adriatic Sea. Her pillars and palaces pierced the sky. Gondolas slipped through the canals that took the place of principle streets. Ships laden with treasure huddled at her wharves. People thronged her bridges and squares and jabbered in many languages in her markets.

In 1253, two brothers set sail from this magic place. Their names were Nicolo and Maffeo Polo. They were not rich men, but they had high hopes for the trip they were making. In the hold of their ship lay grain, salted meat, wood, iron, and woven goods. They planned to trade this merchandise in the eastern capital of Constantinople. That, they thought, should help build their fortunes.

Neither man's wife went with him. Travel was simply too dangerous in those days. Nicolo and Maffeo themselves planned to sail in convoy with other ships. That was the best way to guard against pirate raids. Besides, Nicolo's wife was expecting a baby. Their little boy was born in 1254. He was called Marco after Saint Mark, patron saint of Venice. He would not see his father for fifteen years. The trip east turned out to be a long one.

Unfortunately, we do not know much about Marco's childhood. At some point his mother died. But he had an Aunt Flora on his father's side and several cousins as well. Italian families took care of one another, so Marco probably moved in with his relatives.

Chances are he did not get much formal education, although he did learn to read and write some Italian. Most Venetian boys of that time picked up what knowledge they had from life in the city. Marco would have been no exception.

He could spend hours just wandering along the wharves. There he could see ships from all over Europe, India, Asia Minor, and North Africa. He could touch smooth, creamy ivory and smell exotic spices or stare at slaves from Russia, Turkey, Africa, and the Tartar tribes. Many people then knew that slavery was wrong. But slaves brought such high prices—especially young girls. And Venice's chief goal was to make money.

Venice sat in the perfect spot to do this, right between East and West. Travelers passed through her on their way to many other places. Her merchants had access to almost any country in Europe and the lands along the eastern Mediterranean. Her climate was good and she did not get involved in many wars. No wonder she was known as the Queen of the Adriatic.

But Venice had a spiritual side too. Much of her religious

life centered around old Saint Mark's Church, which stood on one side of the Piazza San Marco (Saint Mark's Square). The original building had burned down in 976. But this one had stood in its place since 1094 and held the remains of Saint Mark himself, miraculously stolen from Egypt where the saint had been killed.

With his friends, young Marco Polo must have drifted into the church and gazed at the rich mosaics, gleaming with gold and glowing colors. There he could see the stories of the Creation, of Noah, Joseph, Moses, and other Old Testament figures. From other pictures he could learn about Jesus' life and teachings. He could stare at the Pala d'Oro, an altarpiece made of gold, silver, and thousands of pearls, rubies, emeralds, sapphires, and other precious gems.

Marco and his friends probably took part in *La Sensa* too. During this Ascension Day feast, the doge, ruler of Venice, traveled in his grand barge to Lido, the city's outermost island. Around him floated thousands of other boats and gondolas, crammed with eager sightseers.

At Lido, the bishop of Castello blessed a special golden ring. Then the doge threw the ring into the Adriatic and cried, "We wed thee, O sea, in token of the true and perpetual dominion of the Most Serene Venetian Republic." After that came a church service, a reception, a state dinner, and an eight-day street fair in Saint Mark's Square.

When he was fourteen, Marco would have attended the

installation of Lorenzo Tiepolo, new doge of Venice. First there was a parade of boats past the doge's palace. Then the parade on land began. In it marched the craftsmen, each dressed according to his guild and profession. The furriers wore furs and the cloth workers cloth. The glassmakers carried flasks and goblets and the lantern makers lanterns full of birds (which they let go). Richest of all were the goldsmiths, draped with jewels of every color. Of course there was also music—trumpets and other instruments and singing children. That festival went on for seven days.

Marco probably learned the most, though, from watching people as they went about their daily lives. At the Arsenal he would see how they could work together to make a product quickly and efficiently.

The Arsenal was built on two islands with a lagoon in the middle. On both sides of the lagoon stood workers at the Arsenal windows. The hull of a new ship was towed in from one end of the lagoon. As she floated along, the workers handed out of the windows the various parts she needed—cordage, arms, and so on. By the time she reached the other end of the lagoon, she was fully equipped. The whole process could take place in less than an hour. It was a thirteenth-century assembly line.

Marco also watched people as they hurried along the streets. Many were businessmen, rushing to appointments. Some were noblemen, their noses in the air. Since the streets were not paved, noble ladies in elegant dresses had trouble keeping the mud off their skirts. For a while they solved this problem by wearing clogs on their feet. But some of the clogs were three feet high. Ladies could seriously injure themselves falling off them. So eventually the city passed a law prohibiting high clogs.

Beggars and pickpockets, lepers and prostitutes also swarmed the streets and squares of Venice. There was plenty of crime, and criminals had to bear their cruel punishments publicly. A thief could have his hands cut off or his eyes torn out. A murderer was beheaded, burned, or cut into quarters. People who committed less serious crimes might be hung in a wooden cage from Saint Mark's bell tower or forced to wear around their neck a board announcing what they had done.

No one—not even the richest people—smelled very good. Venetians did not put much stock in bathing in those days. The few who had underwear wore it, but never washed it. The really rich might splash on some perfume, but its fragrance just mixed with the less pleasant ones.

None of this bothered Marco. Smells were a part of life. After all, everyone threw their garbage and waste into the streets. And the only street cleaners around were the pigs from the monastery of Saint Anthony of Padua.

No doubt some of Marco's favorite people were the sailors he met during those hours spent on the wharves. They had some strange tales to tell, tales of pirates and smugglers and faraway lands. Marco must have drunk in those tales. Had his father played any part in them? he must have wondered. Was his father still alive? Would he ever come home?

Chapter 2

THE MISSING FATHER

Nicolo and Maffeo first steered their ship southeast, through the Adriatic. Then they headed northeast, past the Greek islands in the Aegean Sea and into the Sea of Marmora. All in all, it would take them thirty or forty days to reach the great city of Constantinople.

The wooden ship was hot and slimy and smelled of bilge water and decay. Rats and roaches roamed freely below deck. The best place to sleep was in the open air under an awning. Food consisted of salted meat, hard black biscuits, cheese, onions, garlic, vinegar, and vegetables that quickly spoiled. Plenty of fish swam in the seas, but cooking them on a wooden ship was too dangerous. When they felt thirsty, the Polos could choose between sour wine and smelly water.

But at last they arrived at Constantinople. It must have been worth the trip, because they stayed for six years. No one knows exactly what they did. Probably they traded, bartered, bought and sold various items, then repeated the whole process again. They had come to make money and did not intend to leave until they were satisfied.

After a while, though, Constantinople no longer seemed a safe place to live and work. Latins and Greeks fought over control of the city. Venetians and Genoese both wanted to control the seas. Nicolo and Maffeo shook their heads, exchanged their money for jewels, and moved on to Sudan in the Crimea.

But business there was not good either. So again the Polos decided to travel on. At the moment they could not go back to Venice. Pirates infested the seas and bandits were as thick as mosquitoes on land. Why not head farther east? the Polos asked themselves. Many tribes, such as the Mongols, lived in those distant places. A smart merchant could earn plenty trading wood, skins, salt, and even slaves.

Not long before, no traveler would have dared venture into Mongol lands. In the late twelfth and early thirteenth centuries, the terrible Genghis Khan had been on the rampage, conquering one country after another, burning, looting, and butchering millions of people.

But by the early 1260s, Genghis Khan was dead. His grandson, Kublai Khan, ruled the Mongol lands, which stretched from Hungary east to the Pacific Ocean and from the Indian border north to the Arctic Ocean. Now the Mongols obeyed the *Pax Tatarica*, an agreement that guaranteed the safety of travelers. They wanted merchants to visit them with goods and news from the rest of the world.

So the Polo brothers went east on horseback until they reached Bolgara, a town ruled by Barka Khan, another of Genghis' grandsons. He was happy to see them and, for some reason, they gave him all their jewels. This turned out to be a good investment. In return, Barka gave the Polos gifts worth twice as much.

They spent a year trading these gifts and getting still richer. Then they decided it was time to go home. They had been gone eight years. But before they could leave Bolgara, Barka Khan and his cousin, Hulaku, began fighting. This meant that the road to Constantinople was no longer safe.

"Well, let's circle around and go home another way," thought the brothers. They piled their goods into two-wheeled carts called arabas and set off. First they journeyed to the city of Oucaca, then into rough country and a desert that took them seventeen days to cross. By the time they got to the city of Bokhara, they felt overjoyed to see civilization again. Besides, Bokhara was a marvelous place to trade, full of treasures from China.

Unfortunately, while they were there, more battles broke out among neighboring tribes. This meant they could not go west to Venice or even east to China. They were stuck in Bokhara and there they stayed for three years.

Peace had barely settled again when a messenger came to the city from Kublai Khan himself. He had heard about the two Westerners in Bokhara. Would they mind coming with his messenger to his capital? He wanted to meet them.

"You will have great profit from it and great honor," the messenger assured them.

If the brothers had had any doubts, this erased them. They went. It was no small journey either. For a whole year they traveled, thousands of miles to the east and northeast. They crossed deserts and mountains, fought their way through winter storms and summer heat. Often they stayed with wandering Mongol tribes. These were tough people who slept in felt tents, believed that cleanliness was a sin, and loved to drink koumiss, fermented mare's milk. The Polos must have been hardy individuals just to survive.

No one knows exactly where they found Kublai Khan. He might have been in his old capital city, Karakorum, or in his new one, Khanbalik (Peking). Or he might have been at his summer palace at Shangtu. In any case, he was delighted to meet the Polos and "beamed with the greatest graciousness."

Then, after feeding them and giving them time to rest, he let loose a torrent of questions. What about the Western rulers? What were they like? How did they govern? Did they get along with one another? What sort of manners did they have? And what about "Master the Apostle" (the pope) and the church?

It was the Western church that most interested Kublai Khan. His mother was a Christian, and he wanted to learn all he could about the beliefs of her religion. In fact, he had a mission for the Polo brothers, if they would accept it. He wanted them to be his messengers to the pope. They would have his personal token for safe-conduct, a golden tablet bearing his seal, to get them back to Italy. On it were the words, "By the strength of the eternal heaven, holy be the Khan's name. Let anyone who does not pay him reverence be killed."

The Polos were to ask the pope to send Kublai one hundred scholarly men who knew all about Christianity. If these men could convince him that their faith was better than worshiping idols, he and all his subjects would join the church. Furthermore, he wanted the brothers to return and bring him some oil from the lamp at Jesus' tomb in Jerusalem. This oil was supposed to cure diseases of the body and the soul.

So Nicolo and Maffeo turned around and headed west again. At first Cogotal, one of Kublai's men, traveled with them. But he soon became ill and could not go on. For three years the brothers struggled across Asia on their own. At last they reached Armenia and from there sailed to Acre in Syria.

In Acre they heard bad news. Pope Clement IV had died the previous year and a new pope had not yet been chosen. Now what were they to do with the khan's message? He expected them back with an answer as soon as possible.

Wait until a new pope is elected, advised Teobaldo of Piacenza, a papal representative. That is all you can do.

The Polo brothers agreed. But they saw no point in waiting in Acre. They might as well go back to Venice and stay with their families. Off they sailed and in 1269 returned to their home city.

Nicolo's wife was dead, he learned. But he had a fine, fifteen-year-old son waiting for him. And for the first time, Marco Polo met his father.

Chapter 3

A SLOW BEGINNING

Soon Marco's head was stuffed with new tales of strange and marvelous things. But these tales, he knew, were true. His father and uncle had seen all the wonders of which they spoke. What a journey they must have had!

Now, though, the travelers found themselves in Venice, waiting for the cardinals to elect a new pope. Not that the waiting was all bad. Nicolo married again and at last Marco lived in a real home complete with father and mother.

But the election dragged on for one year, then another. What must the khan be thinking? wondered Nicolo and Maffeo. Were they losing their chance to make the fortune he had promised them?

Finally they decided not to wait any longer. They would sail back to Acre and see what happened there. But they would have a new traveling companion on this journey. Marco was now seventeen—a man. Of course he must come along. He would be a big help.

So, in 1271, two seasoned travelers and one excited Marco set sail for the Mediterranean and Acre. Once again Nicolo left a pregnant wife behind. Marco must have felt very glad that *he* wasn't the unborn baby this time.

He probably also felt a little nervous. He had heard some frightening stories about sea monsters in the Mediterranean. Some, it was said, were a mile long with teeth like beams. They had been known to swim right up to a ship and take a bite out of it.

Fortunately the Polos did not meet any of these monsters on their voyage. They sailed safely into port at Acre, stronghold of the Crusaders. It was a glorious city, built of great square stones. Knights and princes paraded through the streets, dressed in silver and gold. Merchants—both Italian and foreign—flourished. But for once the Polos weren't interested in trade. They hurried to meet again with the papal representative, Teobaldo.

May we go on to Jerusalem to get some of the holy oil for the khan? they asked him.

Teobaldo agreed and the travelers left right away for the port of Joppa. From there they had to journey overland to Jerusalem. As Marco gazed for the first time at the Holy City, he must have thought it was well worth the effort. Here were so many of the places he had learned about from the mosaics at Saint Mark's. Here was Solomon's Temple, the Garden of Gethsemane, the hill where Jesus' cross once stood.

But it was to the site of Jesus' tomb that the Polos made their way. It was a cave, about eight feet long and eight feet wide. Marble now covered the outside, but pilgrims stooping through the small door found bare rock on the inside. The shelf where Jesus' body had lain was on the right.

Above the sepulcher burned a beautiful lamp. Legend said that Jesus' friends, Martha and Lazarus, had placed it there. Supposedly it had remained lit since that time, with one exception. Each Good Friday, the lamp went out at nine o'clock in memory of Jesus' crucifixion. Each Easter Sunday, it lit itself again at the hour Jesus rose from the dead. It was oil from this lamp that Kublai Khan wanted.

The Polos bought some, then returned to Acre to check with Teobaldo again. Pope or no pope, they really must get back to the khan, they felt. So Teobaldo gave them some official letters, explaining why the brothers had not been able to do exactly what the khan wished. He also promised to send word as soon as a new pope was chosen.

On they went to Laias (Ayas) in Lesser Armenia. But a political uprising had blocked the roads leading from the city and again they had to wait. This turned out to be a piece of luck. While they were still in Laias, a messenger arrived from Teobaldo. He himself had been elected pope and wanted them to return to Acre right away.

The king of Armenia provided their transportation this time on an armed galley. As far as he was concerned, these Polos were important men. The new pope, who chose as his name Gregory X, welcomed them with honor, had a feast prepared for them, and gave them his special blessing.

Unfortunately, he could not find one hundred scholarly men to send back to the khan with them. But he did turn up two Dominican friars, Fra Guglielmo di Tripoli and Fra Nicolo da Vicenza. With these two priests, plus jewels, crystal vases, and other gifts for Kublai Khan, the Polos again returned to Laias.

The caravan routes seemed clear now, and they headed deeper into Armenia. But they had not gone far when they learned that the Saracens were raiding the countryside ahead.

The Polos had faced dangers before—and this time they had letters from the pope as well as Kublai Khan's golden tablet to protect them. They decided to go on.

But the two Dominicans disagreed. Frankly, they were terrified. When they heard that a group of Knights Templars were nearby, they felt overwhelmed with relief. Take us with you back to the coast, they pleaded.

One of the knights' jobs was to protect pilgrims, so they agreed. The grateful priests left their letters and gifts for the khan with the Polos and fled.

Chapter 4

THE LONG JOURNEY

Although Laias was definitely a foreign city, Marco could still rub shoulders with plenty of Italian traders—both Venetian and Genoese. But as the Polos continued their journey into Lesser Armenia, he began to observe new and different kinds of people. He was not always impressed.

"In former times its gentry were esteemed expert and brave soldiers," he wrote about Lesser Armenia. "But at the present day they are great drinkers, pusillanimous [cowardly], and worthless."

From Lesser Armenia, the Polos traveled into Turkomania (today Anatolia in eastern Turkey). Here Marco marveled at the horses, mules, handsome carpets, and fine silks.

Next came Greater Armenia where Mount Ararat towered almost seventeen thousand feet into the sky. Atop this mountain, Marco knew, Noah's ark had finally come to rest. But so much snow covered its upper slopes that no one could climb to the top to search for the ark. (No one did climb Ararat until 1829. Those first explorers found no trace of an ark, but later ones did find fossilized wood.)

In Zorzania (today part of Georgia in the Soviet Union), Marco stared at a geyser gushing oil. It took many camels to carry all that oil away, he noticed. But people didn't use it for food. Instead they rubbed it on skin rashes—their own and their camels'—and burned it for light.

He should not have been so surprised. The Egyptians, Persians, and Romans had used petroleum many centuries before. They burned it for heat and light and even waterproofed with it. But the people in Europe had forgotten much that their ancestors had known.

In the city of Mosul, the Polos saw the finely-woven cloth still called muslin today. Marco was also fascinated by the Nestorian Christians there. They took their name from Nestorius, who had once been chief bishop of Constantinople. But in 431 he was deposed for his beliefs, and his followers gradually moved eastward. Some even began a church in China as early as 638.

Although Marco wrote about the city of Baghdad, it is not certain that the Polos actually visited it. Still, Marco did hear a miraculous tale about the area and was eager to share it.

A cruel caliph who ruled Baghdad wanted to harm the Christians living there. He had heard that the Bible said anyone with faith the size of a mustard seed could move a mountain. So he said that one of the Baghdad Christians must do just that at the end of ten days. Otherwise they all must become Muslims or be killed.

For eight days the Christians prayed. Then an angel came

in a vision to a bishop. A cobbler with one eye could help them, said the angel. They found the cobbler and, on the tenth day, went to the mountain with him. The man fell on his knees and prayed. Sure enough, with great rumblings the mountain picked itself up and moved a full mile away.

Many of the caliph's people became Christians on the spot. Some said the caliph did too—but secretly.

Next the Polos arrived in Tabriz, the greatest pearl market in the world. After that came Saba in Persia. Here, Marco said, he saw the tombs of the three Wise Men, Caspar, Melchior, and Balthasar, who had visited the infant Jesus. He heard several legends about them too.

Marco had high praise for Persia, including horses, donkeys, grain, fruits, wild game, military equipment, beautiful embroidery done by the women and young people, and turquoises. (The word "turquoise" means "Turkish stone.")

He was not so happy with the mountain pass they had to cross after leaving the Persian city of Kerman. That pass was ten thousand feet high and cold. On the other side, though, stretched a hot plain. There dates, pomegranates, and quinces grew, and turtledoves cooed. Marco also saw strange, humped oxen (zebu) and sheep with tails that weighed as much as thirty pounds and were good to eat.

The Polos next passed into a section of Persia overrun with bandits known as Karaunas, "who scour the country and plunder every thing within their reach." According to

Marco, this robber tribe had been to India and there learned how to turn day to night. For safety's sake, the Polos joined up with a larger caravan for travel through the region.

Nevertheless, they were attacked during a dust storm (which did seem to turn day to night). While the Polo group managed to escape to a nearby village, the rest of the caravan were not so fortunate. Some were murdered and the others sold into slavery.

The next part of their journey, the Polos had decided, should be taken by sea. So they headed down from the Plateau of Iran and into the city of Hormuz on the Persian Gulf. None of them liked Hormuz. The summer air was "unwholesome" and the hot winds so deadly that the local people stood in water up to their chins until they stopped blowing. While the Polos were there, Marco says, sixty-five hundred soldiers were caught outside the city during a windstorm. Every one of them suffocated. When the people of Hormuz tried to bury them, the corpses crumbled apart.

Marco did not care for the food in Hormuz either. For the most part, people ate salted fish and dates. True, their date wine was delicious. But it gave foreigners diarrhea.

Worst of all, though, were the ships. These were made of wood so hard that nails could not be driven into it. So wooden pegs bound with coconut yarn held the boards together. Definitely not seaworthy, the Polos said to one another, and turned back for Kerman again.

Next their journey led them across a huge salt desert whose green water was too bitter and salty to drink. Finally they reached Tunocain, a city whose women Marco found, "in my opinion . . . the most beautiful in the world."

The same district had once been home to the Hashishin (Assassins), a Muslim sect fanatically devoted to their leader, the "Old Man of the Mountain." There were a series of these leaders between 1090 and 1256. They drugged their men with hashish (a form of cannabis), promised them paradise, and then commanded them to murder various important people. By the time the Polos arrived in Tunocain, the Assassins no longer followed their grisly trade. But many still lived in the hills.

From Tunocain, the Polos went on to Sapurgan, then to Balkh, one of the oldest and once most beautiful cities in Asia. But Genghis Khan had slaughtered its people and burned it to the ground in 1222 and much of it was still charred ruins.

Beyond a plain, the Polos came to a mountain range that produced pure white salt. On the other side of the mountains they found the province of Badakhshan with ruby, sapphire, and lapis lazuli mines. Here, Marco says quite calmly, he was sick for nearly a year. At last someone advised him to go up into the mountains where the air was supposed to be especially pure. He got well almost at once.

After that gap in their journey, the Polos plodded on to the

Pamirs, where three mountain ranges came together. This area was sometimes called "the roof of the world." They saw sheep with horns up to four-and-a-half feet long (which were later named *Ovis poli* in Marco's honor). Birds could not fly to the tops of these mountains, and cooking fires gave less heat. On the other side lay Kashgar and the far edges of China, then known as Cathay.

In Yarkand, Marco noticed that many people had goiter. He suspected that their drinking water caused the problem. In Khotan, he watched men dig jade from dry riverbeds. The desert people beyond Khotan shocked him. It seemed that when a man left home for a long trip, his wife could take a temporary husband and he could take a temporary wife.

Soon, though, the Polos reached a desert where no people lived. After a week of rest at Lop (Charklik), they set out for a thirty-day journey across the great Gobi. Twenty oases along the way were supposed to help travelers. But sometimes their water was not fit to drink.

Besides, people said, the desert teemed with evil spirits. These could sing to travelers in strange voices and show them pictures of things that did not exist. Science now tells us that the "songs" are the sounds of shifting sands and the "pictures" mirages caused by heat waves. But they were pretty terrifying to thirsty travelers of an earlier day.

The Polos survived all these dangers, though, and stumbled at last into Shachow (today called Tunhuang). People here worshiped idols, Marco saw, and sometimes kept dead bodies around for six months. No one got buried until the astrologers said the time was right.

In Chinghintalis Marco saw how asbestos was produced. People back home thought it was the wool of salamanders. Marco could hardly wait to tell them the truth.

For some reason, Nicolo and Maffeo ended up spending a year in the city of Kanchow. Apparently business was good there. Then they went on through the kingdom of Tangut where people looked Oriental. Marco made careful note of that. But he was especially intrigued by the yaks with their fine wool.

"Here are found many fine cattle," he wrote, "that, in point of size, may be compared to elephants. Their color is a mixture of white and black, and they are very beautiful to the sight."

At last, three-and-a-half years after they began their journey, the Polos met some of Kublai Khan's men. The great leader had heard they were drawing near and wanted the remaining part of their trip to be as pleasant as possible. So for the last forty days, the Polos traveled with an escort. Finally they reached Shangtu, the khan's summer residence north of Peking, and entered the palace gates.

Bringing the marvels of India to the khan

Chapter 5

POMP AND PLEASURES

> In Xanadu did Kubla Khan
> A stately pleasure-dome decree:
> Where Alph, the sacred river, ran
> Through caverns measureless to man
> > Down to a sunless sea.
> So twice five miles of fertile ground
> With walls and towers were girdled round:
> And there were gardens bright with sinuous rills,
> Where blossomed many an incense-bearing tree;
> And here were forests ancient as the hills,
> Enfolding sunny spots of greenery.

In 1798, the English poet, Samuel Taylor Coleridge, read Samuel Purchas' version of what Marco had written about the khan's summer palace at Shangtu (Xanadu). He then fell asleep and, in a dream, wrote the poem "Kubla Khan: Or, a Vision in a Dream." When he awoke, he scribbled down his dream poem as fast as he could. Unfortunately, someone interrupted him and he forgot most of it. But what he did get down remains one of the great poems of the English language.

Of course Marco couldn't begin to imagine that what he saw would inspire an English poet hundreds of years later. But it was certainly amazing enough.

The palace itself was built of stone and marble, with gilded rooms and halls. A great wall around it enclosed sixteen square miles of parkland. "Within the bounds of this royal park," wrote Marco, "there are rich and beautiful meadows, watered by many rivulets, where a variety of animals of the deer and goat kind are pastured."

Also within the park stood the "pleasure dome" of which Coleridge wrote.

"In the center of these grounds, where there is a beautiful grove of trees, he has built a royal pavilion," Marco said, "supported upon a colonnade of handsome pillars, gilt and varnished. Round each pillar a dragon, likewise gilt, entwines its tail, whilst its head sustains the projection of the roof.... The roof is of bamboo cane, likewise gilt, and so well varnished that no wet can injure it.... The building is supported on every side (like a tent) by more than two hundred very strong silken cords.... The whole is constructed with so much ingenuity of contrivance that all the parts may be taken asunder, removed, and again set up, at his majesty's pleasure."

The khan "honorably and graciously" welcomed his visitors from Venice. As soon as they kowtowed to him ("kowtow" means "knock head" on the ground), he told them to get up and asked them about their trip. He especially wanted to know how their meetings with the pope had gone.

Nicolo and Maffeo told him all they could and gave him the gifts and letters from Pope Gregory, as well as the oil from Jerusalem. The khan seemed quite satisfied. Then he noticed Marco and asked who he was.

"That is your servant, and my son," replied Nicolo.

"He is welcome, and it pleases me much," said the khan. He immediately had Marco listed as one of his attendants of honor. Then everyone settled down to a huge feast.

In the days ahead, life at Shangtu must have seemed like a luxurious dream to the Polos, especially after their strenuous journey. Kublai Khan had chosen this spot because of its comfortable temperatures during the summer months. Should a storm blow up, he could always summon his magicians. These Buddhist lamas, mostly from Tibet, could climb to the palace roof and chase bad weather from the royal grounds, Marco said. They could also cause a goblet of wine to fly ten feet across the dining hall to the khan's hand. When he'd drunk the wine, the goblet flew back.

Marco did not care for these magicians, though. He said, "they exhibit themselves in a filthy and indecent state. . . . They suffer their faces to continue always uncleansed by washing and their hair uncombed, living altogether in a squalid style." Furthermore, they ate the bodies of executed criminals—"a beastly and horrible practice."

Kublai Khan was addicted to hunting, although he never worked too hard at it. (He was, after all, nearly sixty when Marco met him. He also suffered from gout.) In his park he used either falcons or small cheetahs to bring down game. Outside the park, he lay on a couch in a little house that was covered on the outside with lion skins and on the inside with gold cloth. This house perched on the backs of four elephants. Ten thousand falconers rode with the khan, and he merely watched as they loosed their hawks on the prey. Then a thousand other servants retrieved the hawks after the hunt was over. Dogs, cheetahs, and lynxes were used to hunt deer. Tigers went after boars, bears, and wild oxen. Eagles were specially trained to kill wolves.

A city of tents traveled along with the hunters. When the chase was over, the khan and his men relaxed in them with their ladies. The main tent alone, according to Marco, held at least a thousand people.

But Shangtu was just for June, July, and August. During other periods of the year, Kublai Khan and his court spent time in the capital of Khanbalik, which stood just north of present-day Peking. Marco thought Khanbalik was a splendid city. It was perfectly square with wide, straight streets dividing it into neat blocks. Although many people lived in the city, there was none of the clutter of Venice. Instead, lovely homes each boasted a garden and a courtyard.

A wall forty-five feet high and over forty-five feet wide at the bottom surrounded Khanbalik. Inside the city, another wall enclosed the royal buildings and gardens. Carved golden dragons and colorful paintings of birds, animals, and hunters covered the palace walls. Its varnished roof shone red, blue, green, and purple.

Other buildings housed Kublai Khan's four wives and their courts. In still others lived his concubines. (He got thirty to forty new ones each year.) Nearby rose an artificial hill, a mile round, over a hundred feet high, and planted with evergreen trees. When life became too much for the khan, he retreated to a pavilion at the top of this hill to rest for a while.

Banquets at the palace made a big impression on Marco. Guests had to lower their voices and start looking humble while they were still half a mile away. Before they entered the palace, they had to take off their own shoes and put on white leather slippers. On very special occasions, the khan even supplied their clothes, including suits of gold and expensive gems. Men always carried small vases with lids, in case they had to spit.

As many as six thousand people could sit down in the banquet hall at one time. The khan's own place was on a raised platform with a table full of beverages nearby. His favorite drink was koumiss, but his was not made from the fermented milk of just any mare. It came from a herd of pure white ones.

A royal sip of koumiss was a spectacle all by itself. First a servant with a golden veil over his mouth brought the goblet. (The veil was to keep the servant's breath from polluting the taste of the liquor.) Then, as the drink approached the khan's lips, musicians played and everyone fell to their knees. There they stayed until the khan had finished. Since he was known to drink a lot, many courtiers must have had calluses on their knees.

The more time Marco spent at court, the more he learned. Eventually he could speak four new languages and understand which were proper manners and which were not. Kublai Khan kept his eye on the young man and was pleased with what he saw.

"Finding him thus accomplished," Marco wrote about himself, "his master was desirous of putting his talents for business to the proof and sent him on an important concern of state to a city named Karazan..."

Chapter 6

THE STORY OF THE KHANS

Marco spent seventeen years as a highly favored servant of Kublai Khan. It may seen surprising that the ruler would give so much power to a foreigner. But it made sense.

First, many of the khan's subjects were people whom the Mongols had conquered. Better to trust a foreigner than a conquered subject, thought Kublai. Second, as a European merchant, Marco knew far more than most of the Mongols at court. It was not long before that they had been simple, wandering tribesmen. Kublai's grandfather, Genghis Khan, had changed all that.

Genghis was born around 1162, son of a clan chieftain called Yesukai. His parents named him Temuchin. Their tribe was not very large, and their life was much like that of the tribes around them. They survived by herding cattle, sheep, and goats on the harsh Mongolian plains. Bone-chilling winds swept over them in winter, and a fierce sun scorched them in summer. Only spring brought gentle weather to the Mongols—and it did not last long.

When the Mongols' animals had thoroughly grazed one area, the tribe moved on to another, riding their sturdy little ponies. Their homes went right along with them. These were large, round, felt tents, called yurts. The women of the tribe made the felt by beating wet sheep's wool with sticks. Then they pressed the tangled fibers into cloth and tied it behind their horses. As the horses dragged the felt along, the grass polished it until it shone. Next the women coated it with tallow or cow's milk. This helped waterproof it.

Finally they stretched the felt over light wooden frames and tied it in place with horsehair cords to form a yurt. Beaten cow dung covered with sand made a good floor, although richer Mongols added a rug too. A few benches, a chest or two, and some household tools served as furnishings. Smoke from the dung fire in the middle of the tent escaped through a hole in the roof.

Such a home was not luxurious. But it could easily be picked up, settled on the platform of a cart, and hauled off to new grazing lands.

Then, when the herds had plenty to eat again, the Mongol tribesmen could go hunting. Meat formed the main part of their diet, and they would eat almost anything that moved—including rats.

Another favorite pastime of the Mongol men was fighting other tribes. Often they increased their wealth—or captured their wives—this way. The Mongols believed in a Supreme Being, but they did not pay much attention to him. A medicine man tried to drive out the evil spirits that caused their illnesses. Sometimes he also told their fortunes from burnt sheep bones. That was all they needed of religion. The world they knew was a tough, heartless place. Why should they value human life?

After a hard day of hunting or warring, the men gathered around camp fires and danced. Drums, guitars, and fiddles provided their music. If they wanted a longer rest, they simply laid around their yurts all day and drank koumiss.

Mongol women did not lead an easy life either. Besides making felt, they had to preserve foods, such as milk, butter, and meat. They sewed hides into bags, shoes, and clothing. They tended the herds and, of course, bore and raised children. In a pinch, they could also kill wild animals that threatened their flocks or jump on a horse and fight in a battle.

This was the world into which Temuchin was born. When he was still a boy, enemy tribesmen killed his father and many of his own people sneaked off to join the enemy. But Yesukai's widow would not stand for that. She chased after the deserters and forced them to return. Her son was going to be chieftain or else.

Young Temuchin agreed with her. By the time he turned seventeen, he had led his people on many raids. Tribe after tribe either joined him or was wiped out. Once they were under his power, he organized the Mongols into regiments. Then he set out to make new conquests.

In 1206, at the age of forty-four, Temuchin stood at Karakorum before chieftains from all over the Mongol territories. They fell on their faces in his honor and called him "Genghis Khan " (the Universal Lord).

Till then the Mongols had paid tribute to the rulers of northern China, the Chin. No more, declared Genghis. He would rather fight the Chin, and fight he did. By 1215, he ruled most of the Chin cities.

Genghis had not planned to attack the lands to his west, though—not until they made him angry. He had sent some Mongol representatives to Persia to discuss trade agreements with the sultan there. All at once, and for no apparent reason, the sultan ordered hundreds of Mongol merchants killed. The khan was furious. He would punish that sultan personally, he vowed.

His raids to the west proved enormously successful from his point of view. Town after town fell before him and he ruthlessly butchered their populations, even the dogs and cats. Horses could graze on the site of a city after Genghis Khan had finished with it.

The Persian sultan died in 1221 before Genghis could reach him. But he was able to kill the man's sons and give his daughters to Mongol princes as concubines. He had his revenge. But he could no longer be satisfied. The smell of blood drove him on to yet more slaughter.

"The greatest joy a man can know," he once said, "is to conquer his enemies and drive them before him; to ride their horses and take away their possessions; to see the faces of those who were dear to them wet with tears; and to clasp their wives and daughters in his arms."

On August 18, 1227, Genghis Khan died at the age of sixty-six. With his last breath, he told his sons how to go on with the conquests. His own place in history was secure. He would be remembered forever as one of the greatest monsters who ever lived.

Genghis' son Ogadai took over after him. Ogadai loved to eat and drink. He had sixty wives. He continued to win battles in China and across Russia. In 1241, his hordes charged through Poland and into Hungary. One group even came close to Venice.

The Europeans shook and trembled before these invaders from the East. Surely they came straight from hell (*Tartarus* in Greek). So they called them Tartars and wondered where they would strike next.

But the Mongols did not strike. Instead, in 1242, they went back to Mongolia. Ogadai had drunk himself to death and they could do nothing until they had a new khan. First came Ogadai's son, Kuyuk. But he soon died and Mangu took his place. By then, various grandsons of Genghis were ruling in various areas. Mangu assigned part of China to his own brother, Kublai.

Kublai, however, did too well. He ruled with justice and kindness instead of bloodshed. It worked. So, in a jealous fit, Mangu called him back and set out to run things his own way. He died, though, before he could accomplish much and once again Kublai stepped in. By then he understood politics. In 1260, at the age of forty-six, he got himself elected khan before anyone else could interfere.

That caused civil war in his family. But Kublai managed to hold on to his power. Soon he was crowned "Son of Heaven." This made him Emperor of China as well as master of many other regions. It was time now, he felt, to settle down and govern the way he thought was best. Unlike his grandfather, Genghis, Kublai Khan intended to be civilized. The ancient culture of the Chinese people would help him reach this goal. So would the work of clever foreigners, such as Marco Polo.

Venice, the Queen of the Adriatic, in the fourteenth century

Constantinople was the gateway to the Orient.

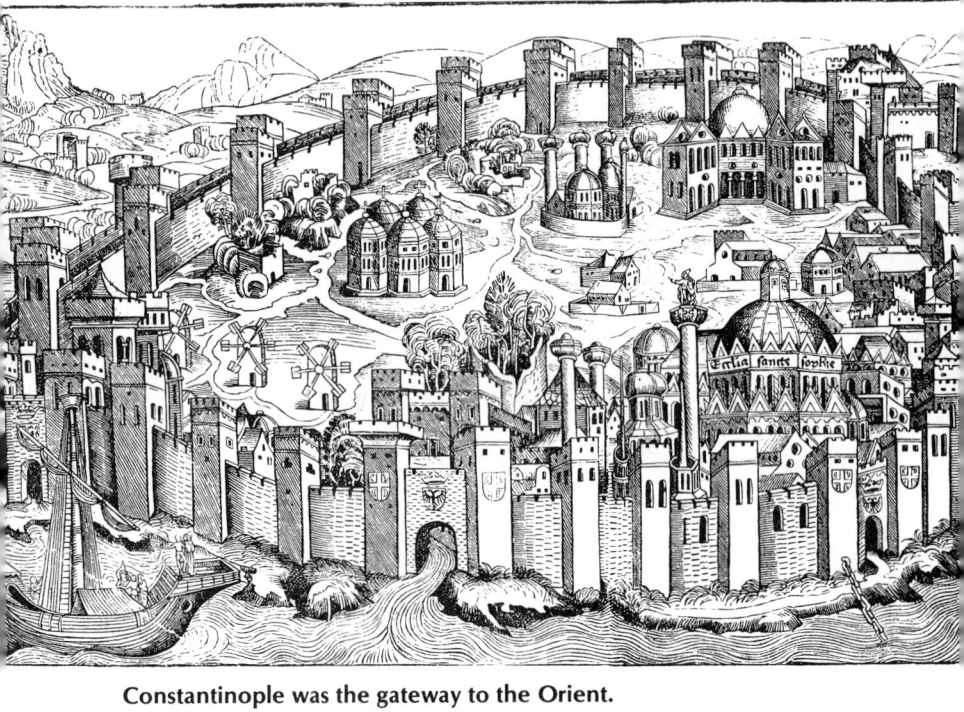

Above: Nicolo and Maffeo Polo meet with Pope Gregory X.

Left: The Polo brothers leave Constantinople for Asia.

Above: The crowning of Genghis Khan

Left: A watercolor of Genghis Khan from the Peking Historical Museum

Nicolo and Maffeo are presented to Kublai Khan.

Above: Kublai Khan traveling

Below: The Imperial Palace in Peking

Marco Polo

Marco Polo being welcomed at the court of Kublai Khan.

Chapter 7

LIFE WITH KUBLAI

By the time Marco began working for the khan, Kublai had already taken advantage of many Chinese discoveries and systems. One at which Marco especially marveled was the use of paper money. In Europe, people still used coins for their transactions. This was so much more convenient.

For some reason, though, Marco did not pay much attention to the fact that the money was *printed*. Although people in China had been printing since the 800s, Europeans did not learn how until the 1400s. Marco could have brought them a valuable tool if he had studied the process.

But he was a merchant and he thought like one. What he did notice right away was how quickly the flimsy paper money wore out. The old bills then had to be traded in at the mint and a 3 percent fee was charged for new ones. What a quick and easy profit for the government, thought Marco.

Marco was also impressed by the khan's mail service, an early version of the pony express. It was another of those Chinese institutions that Kublai adapted for his own purposes. Stations, called yambs, sat at twenty-five to thirty mile intervals along the main roads. An official messenger could gallop into one of these stations, grab some provisions and a fresh horse, and be on his way in no time. Or he could spend the night. Nearby towns kept the stations supplied and some were quite elegant.

All in all, there were at least ten thousand stations with three hundred thousand horses in the khan's territories. Sometimes substations with both foot runners and horses were used at three-mile intervals. In a real emergency, a messenger could go five hundred miles in just one day. No wonder Marco was impressed.

He told in his own words of another Chinese marvel he discovered.

"Throughout this province there is found a sort of black stone, which they dig out of the mountains, where it runs in veins. When lighted, it burns like charcoal, and retains the fire much better than wood; insomuch that it may be preserved during the night, and in the morning be found still burning. These stones do not flame, excepting a little when first lighted, but during their ignition give out a considerable heat."

The burning black stones were coal, which had been used in Britain as far back as the Roman settlements there. But Marco had never seen it before. He watched in amazement as the Chinese used it to heat their baths. Why, people bathed at least three times a week in summer and daily in winter. The Venetians would never believe that!

Because of the astonishing things Marco reported, legends

have grown up about him that are not true. One says that he brought macaroni to Italy from China. He did not. He simply compared a form of pasta the Chinese ate to macaroni or lasagna.

Marco did not bring ice cream to Europe either, as some folks say. Instead, he told about a form of dried milk that the Mongols took with them when they went to war.

The young Venetian spent time observing the khan's methods of ruling his people. Obviously Kublai was a dictator. But he could be very generous when he wanted to be.

"The grand khan sends every year his commissioners to ascertain whether any of his subjects have suffered in their crops of corn from unfavorable weather, from storms of wind or violent rains, or by locusts, worms, or any other plague," wrote Marco. "And in such cases he not only refrains from exacting the usual tribute of that year, but furnishes them from his granaries with so much corn as is necessary for their subsistence, as well as for sowing their land."

In order to have plenty of grain on hand for bad times, the khan bought large quantities during good times and stored it away.

"All his thoughts, indeed," wrote Marco, "are directed to the important object of assisting the people whom he governs, that they may be enabled to live by their labor and improve their substance."

But, he continues, "we must not omit to notice a peculiarity of the grand khan." It seemed that when a herd of sheep or cattle or a ship full of merchandise was struck by lightning, Kublai gave up the percentage due him too. In this case, though, he was thinking of himself. He felt that "God . . . has shown himself to be displeased with the owner of the goods, and he is unwilling that property bearing the mark of divine wrath should enter his treasury."

The khan had a peculiar streak when it came to gambling too. He forbade it. He had conquered these people, he said. Therefore, everything they owned belonged to him. He was not about to have them gambling away his property.

Poor people in Kublai's capital city of Khanbalik knew his kindness as well as the farmers did. When illness or some other misfortune left a family destitute, he gave them food and clothing for as long as they needed it. Marco says he distributed twenty thousand vessels of grain each day. He also set up hospitals, took care of homeless children, and saw to it that they were educated.

Kublai's attitude toward the poor came as a real shock to some of the other Mongols. They were used to driving beggars away from them. "Begone with your complaint of a bad season which God has sent you!" they would cry. "Had he loved you, as it appears he loves me, you would have prospered as I do."

But "the wise men of the idolaters" had told Kublai that

showing kindness to the poor was a good work and pleased their gods. It is not clear whether he wanted to please idols or was simply a shrewd politician. In any case he cared for the poor and, as a result, according to Marco, "the people all adored him as a divinity."

After traveling through the desert, the Polos arrive in "civilization."

Chapter 8

ON THE ROAD

The khan sent Marco on missions because of his business experience and his trustworthiness. But he had a third reason too. Kublai was a curious man. He wanted to know what was going on in the many corners of his realm. Since Marco obviously knew how to use his eyes and ears, he would trust him to bring back the sort of information a ruler needed.

Marco was more than happy to oblige. On each of his trips he made careful notes. Then he told the khan all he had seen and heard.

On his first journey, he traveled into Yunnan province, southwest of Khanbalik. Through valleys, across rivers, and over mountains he trekked. He found a stone bridge so wide that ten horsemen could ride across it abreast. He wandered through cities and rural areas, gazed at castles and at simple homes.

Some of the people he met were farmers. Others tended vineyards whose grapes supplied the interior regions of China. Silkworms fed on the mulberry trees and from them the local people made silk. Citizens of the city of Gouza manufactured "gold tissues and the finest of gauze." The country around the Kara-moran River produced ginger as well as silk. Birds, especially pheasants, thrived there.

"Here likewise grows a species of large cane in infinite abundance," wrote Marco, "some of a foot, and others a foot and a half (in circumference), which are employed by the inhabitants for a variety of useful purposes."

Eventually he arrived in Tibet, "a desolated country." Many of the towns and castles still lay in ruins from the Mongol invasion. Inhabitants had fled and, as a result, wild beasts flourished—especially tigers. These posed a real danger to merchants and other travelers through the area. If the tigers didn't attack them, they might at least go after their horses.

But, says Marco, clever travelers had figured out a way to handle this problem. Each evening they tied large, green bamboo canes together, placed them at a safe distance from their camp, and lit a fire around them. Before long the heat caused the canes to explode with a tremendous noise, "terrifying the wild beasts and making them fly from the neighborhood."

The travelers had to be careful, though, to shackle their horses. Otherwise they would "fly from the neighborhood" too and leave their owners stranded.

Deeper in Tibet, Marco found more people. He didn't like them. "These idolatrous people are treacherous and cruel," he wrote, "and holding it no crime or turpitude to rob, are the greatest thieves in the world." They wore leather, undressed skins, or canvas for clothing and used coral for money. "By their infernal art . . . they cause tempests to arise, accompanied with flashes of lightning and thunderbolts, and produce many other miraculous effects."

People in the province of Kain-du used cakes of salt for money and in Karaian and other regions they used seashells. In Karazan, Marco met up with some terrifying beasts.

"Here are seen huge serpents," he wrote, "ten paces in length, and ten spans in the girth of the body. At the fore part, near the head, they have two short legs, having three claws like those of a tiger, with eyes larger than a fourpenny loaf and very glaring. The jaws are wide enough to swallow a man, the teeth are large and sharp, and their whole appearance is so formidable, that neither man, nor any kind of animal, can approach them without terror."

These "huge serpents" were crocodiles. (We can hardly blame Marco for not getting close enough to notice their hind legs.) They were much prized by hunters in the area, both for their meat and their gall. The gall, mixed with wine, was supposed to be especially useful for treating people who had been bitten by a rabid dog.

Before the khan began to rule this region, its people had a nasty habit of killing travelers who lodged with them, particularly handsome ones "with distinguished valor." They did not do this out of dislike or even to get the travelers' money. They simply wanted their spirits to hover around the house and bring good luck. The khan quickly put an end to that practice.

On the Burmese border, Marco saw people who covered their teeth with gold. The men also had tattooed stripes around their arms and legs.

In this area, as soon as a woman gave birth to a child, she got up and washed and dressed it. Then her husband leaped into bed and stayed there for forty days with the baby while his wife took care of both of them. This was supposed to make the father feel closer to his child. Marco does not say how the women felt.

In Burma, he also learned of a battle that had taken place in 1277 between the Burmese and the Mongols. The Burmese used elephants, each bearing a little enclosure that could hold ten or twelve soldiers on its back. All in all there were sixty thousand Burmese and herds of elephants. The Mongol leader had only twelve thousand men with horses. Furthermore, the horses were frightened by the elephants.

But the Mongol leader had a plan. He told his men to get off their horses and shoot at the elephants with arrows. The elephants ran into some nearby woods where branches knocked off all the enclosures and soldiers. Then the Mongols got back on their horses, chased the Burmese, and killed them.

Pretty clever, thought the khan when he heard about it. But those elephants were not such a bad idea either. From then on, he used elephants in his army too.

In Mien, Marco saw the tomb of a former king. It was two pagodas, one covered with silver and the other with gold. When Kublai conquered this city, he refused to disturb the pagodas. To loot the resting place of the dead, he felt, would be a terrible sin.

The province of Bangala, according to Marco, boasted hordes of magicians as well as oxen almost as tall as elephants. In Kangigu lived a king with four hundred wives. His subjects were also fond of tattoos and covered themselves with pictures of birds and animals. Some died from loss of blood in the process.

Another mission took Marco to Mangi in the southeastern part of China. "The province of Mangi," he wrote, "is the most magnificent and richest that is known in the eastern world." Once again he traveled from city to city, seeing what he could see.

At Yangchow, he says, he served as governor for three years. More likely he was the khan's personal representative. In either case, he had very little to say about Yangchow except that it was "a place of great consequence."

Marco's reports about Sa-yan-fu are also confusing. He says that his father and uncle helped the khan capture the city by showing his workmen how to build mangonels, machines that could throw huge stones. But other records state the Sa-yan-fu fell to Kublai two years before the Polos reached China.

The Yangtze River made a tremendous impression on Marco. He called it "the largest river in the world, its width being in some places ten, in others eight, and in others six miles." At one point he saw fifteen thousand vessels near one city. He wrote down exactly how they were constructed.

But it was the city of Kinsai (today Hangchow) that captured his heart. It was a place, he said, "which might lead an inhabitant to imagine himself in paradise." The city was a hundred miles round with clean, paved streets, canals, and immense squares. Twelve thousand bridges permitted ships to sail through and carts to drive over its waterways.

More than a million and a half families lived in Kinsai. They were served by ten huge markets. There they could buy the meat of wild game or cattle, fish, herbs, and fruit, including pears that weighed as much as ten pounds each.

Around the market squares stood shops selling pearls, trinkets, spices, medicines, and rice wine. Nearby were establishments offering cold baths, which the citizens felt were healthy. Special apartments, though, provided warn water, "for the use of strangers, who, from not being habituated to it, cannot bear the shock of the cold."

Along one side of the city lay a large lake with two islands in the middle. Citizens of Kinsai could use the many pavilions on these islands for their own private celebrations. Or they could climb aboard one of the many pleasure boats that cruised the lake and relax for a while after work.

Marco found most of the homes in Kinsai beautiful. But they were made of wood and sometimes caught fire. Kinsai, says Marco, was ready for such emergencies. A watchman stood on each of the main bridges and when he saw a fire, he beat on a wooden drum. At once all the other watchmen in the area rushed to help him put out the blaze. Meanwhile, inhabitants of the burning building could store their possessions in strategically placed stone towers for safekeeping.

It was not just the sights of Kinsai, though, that made the city special for Marco. He also liked the people.

"The natural disposition of the native inhabitants of Kinsai is pacific [peaceful]," he wrote, "and by the example of their former kings, who were themselves unwarlike, they have been accustomed to habits of tranquility. The management of arms is unknown to them, nor do they keep any in their houses.

"Contentious broils are never heard among them. They conduct their mercantile and manufacturing concerns with perfect candor and probity [honesty]. They are friendly towards each other, and persons who inhabit the same street, both men and women, from the mere circumstance of neighborhood, appear like one family.

"In their domestic manners they are free from jealousy or suspicion of their wives, to whom great respect is shown, and any man would be accounted infamous who should presume to use indecent expressions to a married woman."

It was a first-class city, thought Marco, and he visited it frequently.

Chapter 9

THE GOLDEN WEB

Seventeen years passed as Marco traveled for the khan. For him they were good years. He grew from a young into a middle-aged man, rich in knowledge and experiences. Little is known about his father and uncle during that period. Probably they stayed busy growing rich in other ways. Marco was too eager to tell his own story to spend any time on theirs.

But at last, in 1291, the day arrived when all of the Polos began to dream of returning home. Marco put it like this:

"Our Venetians having now resided many years at the imperial court, and in that time having realized considerable wealth, in jewels of value and in gold, felt a strong desire to revisit their native country, and, however honored and caressed by the sovereign, this sentiment was ever predominant in their minds.

"It became the more decidedly their object, when they reflected on the very advanced age of the grand khan, whose death, if it should happen previously to their departure, might deprive them of that public assistance by which alone they could expect to surmount the innumerable difficulties of so long a journey, and reach their homes in safety..."

So the Polos were homesick. Furthermore, they were afraid of what might happen in the lands between China and home if the khan were to die before they left. Chaos always erupted when a great ruler died and Kublai was now seventy-five. They probably also worried about what might happen to them at court without his protection. They had become rich and powerful men. Surely they had also made some enemies who would act out their jealousy when the khan was no longer there.

In any case, Nicolo approached Kublai "one day when he observed him to be more than usually cheerful." He threw himself at the khan's feet and asked his permission for them to leave.

The khan, says Marco, "appeared hurt at the application, and asked what motive they could have for wishing to expose themselves to all the inconveniences and hazards of a journey in which they might probably lose their lives." If they wanted more riches, he said, he would give them twice what they already had. But he loved them too much to let them leave.

Nicolo took a deep breath and tried again. He had a wife in Venice, he said. By Christian law, he could not forsake her.

The khan saw through that story right away. Nicolo had been home only once in thirty-seven years. At two different times, he had left two wives behind, both pregnant, and he had shown no great interest in getting back to either. No, repeated the khan, he loved the Polos too much to let them go. Further pleas met with the same answer.

He probably did feel real affection for the three Polos. After all, they had been "his" men for a long time. But he would miss their services as much as he would miss their friendship. They had been very useful to him, especially Marco.

So there they sat, caught in a golden web that they had helped spin. Months passed before they saw a glimmer of hope in the form of three messengers from Persia.

Argon, Kublai's grandnephew, was khan of Persia at that time. His beloved wife, Bolgana, had recently died and he wanted a new one from among her relatives in Mongolia. So he sent the three messengers, Uladai, Apusca, and Coja, to ask Kublai to choose a wife for him.

Kublai chose Princess Cocachin, "a damsel aged seventeen, extremely handsome and accomplished." The messengers approved and headed back to Persia with the princess. They had traveled for eight months when they had to stop. Once again Mongol princes were fighting among themselves. The roads were simply too dangerous for the travelers to continue. Wearily they turned around and made their way back to Khanbalik.

Meanwhile, Marco had just returned from a sea voyage to India. The Persians had an idea. Why not ask the Polos to help them get their precious burden home by sea? They met with the Polos, who were delighted with the plan. Once they had gotten as far as Persia, they could easily go the rest of the way to Venice.

The Persians, along with the princess, presented their idea to Kublai. He was not pleased. Everyone could tell that by his face. But he did not have much choice. So he gave in and sent for the Polos.

When they appeared before him, he "addressed them with much kindness and condescension, assuring them of his regard, and requiring from them a promise that when they should have resided some time in Europe and with their own family, they would return to him once more."

Considering Kublai's age, no one must have taken that promise too seriously, except the khan himself. He, though, underlined his trust by making the Polos his ambassadors to the kings of England, France, Spain, and other Christian countries, and to the pope. He gave them two more gold safe-conduct tablets and probably some jewels too. Best of all, he had fourteen ships prepared for their journey.

These, noted Marco with glee, each had four masts and nine sails. Some boasted sixty cabins below and required crews of two hundred fifty men to sail them. All in all they were much better than European ships of the time and the khan had them stocked with two years' worth of provisions.

At last, in the spring of 1292, the Polos set sail from the port of Zayton on the South China Sea. With them went about two thousand people, including the three Persian messengers and Princess Cocachin. They were on their way home.

Kublai Khan had one house that was perched on the backs of four elephants.

Chapter 10

VOYAGE OF WONDERS

For some reason, Marco decided to make a few notes about Japan before going on with his adventures between China and Persia. The fact that he had never been to Japan, which he called Zipangu, did not stop him. He put together a mishmash of tales others told him and ended up with a very strange picture indeed.

Japan, he said, lay about fifteen hundred miles off the coast of Mangi. Its people were fair, well made, civilized, and rich. The king's palace was roofed with gold plate and so were the halls inside the building. The Japanese people owned so many huge pearls that sometimes they put them in the mouths of dead people before they buried them.

These civilized people, he continued, did worship idols. The more arms an idol had, the more powerful they believed it to be. They also ate the bodies of their enemies, after inviting friends and relatives to join them for the feast.

The fact is that Kublai Khan had tried to conquer the island kingdom of Japan. Marco says he failed because his two chief commanders kept bickering between themselves. More likely the Mongol warriors, who had to reach Japan by boat, were not able to fight as well without their horses.

The loss must have rankled and may have given birth to some of the fantastic information Marco later learned.

His own journey now took him first to the kingdom of Champa (part of today's Vietnam). This country was still the khan's territory and each year paid him tribute consisting of twenty large, handsome elephants and a great deal of sweet-smelling wood. Marco had been to Champa before and had discovered that its king was the proud father of 326 children, many of whom grew up to be brave soldiers.

From Champa. the convoy sailed to Java, an island kingdom rich in spices and drugs. Many of these goods were exported to China. As a result, says Marco, "the quantity of gold collected there exceeds all calculation and belief." Java did not belong to the khan, he adds, because of the long and dangerous voyage required to get there.

Past other islands they sailed until they came to Sumatra, which Marco called Java the Lesser. There he visited six of the island's eight kingdoms and saw more strange sights.

In Ferlek, he said, the mountain people ate human flesh. They also spent each day worshiping the first thing they happened to see when they woke up in the morning.

In Basman lived both elephants and rhinoceroses. Perhaps because of its single horn, Marco compared the rhinoceros to the unicorn. They were "quite of a contrary nature," he said. In fact, the rhinoceroses "take delight in muddy pools and are filthy in their habits."

Monkeys with human-looking faces also lived in Basman. Apparently traders had been known to kill and dry these monkeys, then sell them in Europe as the preserved bodies of pigmies. Marco did not approve.

He and his companions had to spend five months in the kingdom of Samara. The southwest monsoon was blowing and they could not sail against it. Unfortunately, "the savage natives" were cannibals, which did not make for a pleasant visit.

For safety's sake, the travelers dug a trench around their camp on shore and posted guards. Eventually, though, they formed some sort of friendship with the natives who brought them coconuts, palm wine, and sago flour made from the pith of a tree. (Later, Europeans refused to believe Marco when he told them such things existed.)

On their way again, Marco found more cannibals in Dragoian and in Lambri, people with hairless tails. (They were probably some form of ape.) At Fanfur, the last kingdom he visited in Sumatra, he noted the production of much fine camphor.

Next the ships came to the Andaman Islands. "The inhabitants are idolaters," wrote Marco, "and are a most brutish and savage race, having heads, eyes, and teeth resembling those of the canine species. Their dispositions are cruel, and every person, not being of their own nation, whom they can lay their hands upon, they kill and eat."

It was obviously not a place to linger and they sailed on, across the Indian Ocean, to Ceylon. Here Marco was impressed by the rubies and other fine gems. The king, he said, owned "the grandest ruby that ever was seen, being a span in length, and the thickness of a man's arm, brilliant beyond description, and without a single flaw."

The khan offered to give the king "the value of a city" for this ruby. But the king said "he would not sell it for all the treasure of the universe," because he had inherited it from those who ruled before him.

On Ceylon stood a high mountain at whose summit was supposed to lie the tomb of the biblical Adam. Many pilgrims climbed to the tomb by means of iron chains placed in the rock. Some years earlier, the khan decided that he wanted some of the remains from the tomb. The king of Ceylon gave his ambassadors "two large back-teeth, together with some of the hair," which Kublai welcomed to Khanbalik "with great pomp and solemnity."

But the idolaters of Ceylon, says Marco, maintained that Adam was not buried in that tomb. Instead, it was the resting place of Sogomonbarchan (Sakyamuni), the Indian prince who became the Buddha.

Sakyamuni, continues Marco, though the son of a king, did not care for earthly pleasures. His father tried to tempt him with women and other delights. He also tried to keep Sakyamuni from learning about old age and death. But one day the prince met an old man and learned the truth. That convinced him that the goods of this life meant nothing. He climbed a tall mountain and lived there like a hermit until his death.

His father then ordered a statue of gold and precious stones erected in Sakyamuni's memory and ordered his subjects to worship it. Sakyamuni himself was reincarnated eighty-four times as various animals. Then he became a god higher than all other gods.

Marco had shown little patience with the Muslim people he met or with idolaters of various sorts. But he seemed to have a soft spot for the Buddha. "For truly if he had been baptized Christian," he wrote, "he would have been a great saint with our Lord Jesus Christ for the good life and pure which he led."

From Ceylon, the ships journeyed on to Malabar on the southwest coast of India. On the way, Marco watched the pearl fishers who dived deep into the sea to fetch their oysters. To protect these divers from sharks during the day, Hindu magicians cast spells on the creatures. At night they removed the spells. Anyone who poached the oyster beds at night deserved to be eaten, they felt.

The people of Malabar, says Marco, "always go naked, excepting that they cover with a piece of cloth those parts of the body which modesty dictates." The king, who had a thousand wives and concubines, did not wear any more clothes than anyone else. But he did drape himself with an immense amount of jewelry, including rings on his fingers and his toes.

When a king died and his body was placed on a funeral pyre for cremation, the men closest to him often jumped into the flames too. They wanted to go on serving him in the next life. Hindu women were expected to do the same thing when their husbands died. Those who refused were "despised and reviled." This custom, known as suttee, continued in India until the nineteenth century.

Sometimes religious fanatics decided to sacrifice themselves to an idol. Their friends carried them through the streets and gave them twelve sharp knives. When they reached the idol, the fanatic would plunge eleven of the knives into various parts of his body, crying, "I devote myself to death in honor of such an idol." Finally he thrust the last knife into his heart and died.

The Hindu people of Malabar, he noticed, considered the cow a sacred animal and would not eat beef. Although they did eat sheep and other beasts and birds, they would not kill them. Instead, they hired a Muslim to do the job for them.

They washed "their whole bodies" twice a day before eating, and each person drank only from his or her own cup. If a stranger wanted a drink and had no cup, they poured the liquid into his hands.

Marco also admired the beds of some of the richer natives.

These were made of cane with curtains that could be pulled shut. "This they do," he wrote, "in order to exclude the tarantulas, which bite grievously, as well as to prevent their being annoyed by fleas and other small vermin." Air, however, "so necessary for mitigating the excessive heat," could pass through the curtains.

If one person in Malabar owed another money and would not pay, the creditor used an unusual method to collect. By law, he could draw a circle around the debtor, who could not step outside it until the debt had been settled.

One day Marco saw the king riding on horseback. Suddenly a foreign merchant darted out and drew a circle around both king and horse. It seemed the king had owed him money for a long time.

The merchant was right, agreed the king. He would not leave the circle until his debt was paid. Onlookers felt very proud to have a king who followed the law.

People who drank wine made from grapes or who sailed the seas were not allowed to testify in court in Malabar. This, says Marco, was because they were thought to be "people of desperate fortunes . . . whose testimony, as such, ought not to be admitted."

North of Malabar, he saw diamond fields and west of them met people of the Brahman and yogi castes. The Brahmans, he said, "are the best and most honorable merchants that can be found. No consideration whatever can induce them to speak an untruth, even though their lives should depend upon it."

The yogis did not wear a stitch of clothing, saying, "there can be no shame in that state of nudity in which they came into the world." They used dried leaves as plates for the little they ate, and slept on the bare ground. Yogis refused to kill anything, "even a fly, a flea, or a louse, believing them to be animated with souls." To Marco's astonishment, some yogis lived to be 150 years old. He felt this must be because of "their temperance and chastity."

From India, the convoy sailed on for Persia. On the way, Marco made notes about a number of islands that he did not visit personally. Two he called the Island of Males and the Island of Females. Only men lived on one and only women on the other, except during March, April, and May, when the men moved in with their wives. Boys stayed with their mothers until they were twelve years old. Then they switched to the Island of Males.

Whoever told Marco about these islands was merely repeating an old tale. They never existed.

Reports he heard about Madagascar were not much better. There, said Marco, lived a huge bird known as a roc. It was supposedly "so large and strong as to seize an elephant with its talons, and to lift it into the air, from whence it lets it fall to the ground, in order that when dead it may prey upon the carcass."

It is true that huge birds once lived on Madagascar. But the roc is a mythical creature, alive only in tales such as those of *The Arabian Nights*.

At last, over two years after they had left China, Marco and his companions sailed into the port of Hormuz in Persia. The first long leg of the Venetians' journey had ended.

Venice, with the rounded dome of St. Mark's in the background behind the Palace of the Doges

Chapter 11

HOMECOMING

It had not been an easy journey. Besides the crew, six hundred people had entered the ships in China. By the time they reached Persia, only eighteen of them remained alive. These included the three Polos, the messenger Coja, and Princess Cocachin. For some reason, all but one of the women and girls on the trip had survived.

Furthermore, the travelers soon learned that Argon had died while waiting for his new bride. Now what would become of the princess? they wondered. Marry her to Argon's son, Ghazan, suggested Argon's brother. The two young people agreed and before long the marriage took place. (Ironically, after all she had been through getting to Persia, Cocachin died less than two years after her marriage.)

Now that they had accomplished their mission, the Polos went on by land to Tabriz where they stayed for nine months. While they were there, they received news from China. Kublai Khan had died.

So, the Polos must have thought, we got away just in time. But they also realized that now they could never return to the eastern kingdoms. Without Kublai's protection, they would no longer be welcome.

Finally they decided to continue westward. Argon's brother, Kaikhatu, gave them four golden safe-conduct tablets of his own. Cocachin, who must also have been at Tabriz, cried to see Marco go. She had learned to like him very much during the years they had been together.

But go he must. With his father and his uncle, he traveled on to Trebizond on the Black Sea. Thanks to Kaikhatu's tablets, they arrived safely. But in Trebizond, disaster struck. No one knows exactly what happened. But it seems that they were robbed either of a lot of money or of many of their goods.

That must have been a bitter loss to the Polos. Here they had journeyed for years through primitive lands. Now, in a city where European traders roamed freely, such a thing had to happen.

Sadly they got on another ship and sailed to Constantinople. After a short stay there, they went on through the Aegean Sea and up the Adriatic to Venice.

There she lay, her towers piercing the sky. They saw Lido and Saint Mark's. There were the harbor, the wharves, and the gondolas. The year was 1295 and they were home at last.

It must have seemed strange to step on Venetian soil after twenty-five years away. They were not the same men who had once lived here either. Nicolo and Maffeo had turned old and gray. Marco himself was now forty-one. All three spoke with eastern accents. They had not had much opportunity to use their native tongue while they were gone.

With them came two young men, Stefano and Giovannino. These were Nicolo's illegitimate sons, born in Asia. With them also came at least one slave, Peter, who belonged to Marco. All the Polos wore ragged clothing. This was the safest way to travel. Anyone who looked too prosperous could be sure of being robbed.

According to one legend, their own relatives did not recognize them. The travelers knocked on the door of the house where their families lived together. The people inside peeked out at them and thought they were strangers. One of those people would have been Maffeo, son of Nicolo's second wife. He had not been born when his father, uncle, and half-brother left Venice.

Eventually, though, Uncle Maffeo's wife must have recognized him. Another legend tells how she longed to get rid of the dreadful clothes he had worn home. One day she gave them to a beggar. When Maffeo found out, he tore his hair, beat his breast, and screamed with rage. All his jewels, he told her, had been sewn inside those clothes.

At last he stopped yelling long enough to figure out a way to get his treasure back. He took a spinning wheel without wool to one of the busiest corners in the city. There he sat for two full days, spinning away at nothing and pretending to be a madman.

People from all over Venice came to see this sight and on

the third day, Maffeo spied a man wearing his rags. Gleefully he jumped to his feet, grabbed the man, and recovered his clothes and the jewels inside.

A third legend says that even after the relatives knew who the travelers were, they did not seem very proud of them. So Marco, Nicolo, and Maffeo decided to teach them a lesson.

They invited everyone to a banquet. Then, during the course of the meal, they each wore three different robes. The first three were of crimson satin, the second three of crimson damask, and the third three of crimson velvet. Finally they dressed themselves in regular clothing. But as they finished with each set of robes, they had them cut up and gave the expensive fabric to their servants. The relatives were horrified at such waste.

But Marco and the others were not done. For their last trick, they brought out their ragged traveling clothes, cut them apart with knives, and poured the jewels hidden in them all over the table. After that, concludes the legend, the relatives treated them with respect.

In fact, suddenly all Venice wanted to honor the Polos. Maffeo became a magistrate. Marco entertained many young men each day, all of whom hung on his every word. People in the streets pointed and stared.

But such peaks of glory never do last long. Soon the novelty wore off and the Polos settled down to life as merchants again.

Chapter 12

A PRISON AND A BOOK

Even before Marco went to China, the people of Venice and the people of Genoa did not get along. Their relationship had not improved during the twenty-five years he was gone either. In fact, it got worse.

It was all a matter of money. Whoever controlled trade on the seas—especially in the eastern Mediterranean—would earn more. Sharing was out of the question. One city must dominate and each was determined to be that city.

In 1295, each sent ships to attack the other's district in Constantinople. Both districts were almost destroyed. Marco was a merchant, so this made him angry. There are two different stories about what happened to him next.

One says he was on a trading mission to Laias with twenty-four other Venetian ships when Genoese galleys attacked. The Venetians lost and many were taken prisoner, including Marco.

The second story has Marco commander of a Venetian galley sent with others to attack the Genoese near the Dalmatian island of Curzola. Marco's ship plunged right into battle. But the others did not follow. So they all lost and Marco, wounded, was hauled off to Genoa.

In either case, the world traveler soon found himself shut up in a tower of the Palazzo del Capitano del Popolo in Genoa. At least he had not been thrown into a dungeon like many other prisoners. But the palazzo was a particularly humiliating place to be. The Genoese had built it from stones of a Venetian palace that once stood in Constantinople. Even its stone lions were Venetian, symbols of Saint Mark.

Marco had a lot of company in prison. The palazzo teemed with men from various cities the Genoese considered enemies. Apparently these men were able to move around and mingle freely. But it didn't do them much good at first. Dialects were so different in the different parts of Italy that they could barely understand one another.

With patience, though, they overcame this handicap. Soon the best moments of the day were those they spent swapping stories and memories of home. For these men, Marco was a gold mine. What tales he could tell! What adventures he had! True, they could not understand all he said. They could not believe all of it either. But who cared? If some of what he told them was not true, well, it still made a good story.

The historian Ramusio says that Marco's tales became so famous throughout Genoa that noble gentlemen came to listen to him too. In payment for the entertainment he gave them, they made sure he had everything he needed.

One day Marco met a prisoner from Pisa. This fellow, Rustichello, was a professional writer. He knew French, the language of educated people throughout Europe. In French he had already written many tales, such as those about King Arthur and the Knights of the Round Table.

Perhaps Marco had the idea first. He was getting a bit weary of repeating his stories again and again. Why not have Rustichello write them down for him? Then at least the educated folk could read them for themselves.

Or maybe Rustichello thought of it. What a rich source of material Marco must have seemed to him. And for once he would be writing about a real, live hero, someone he knew.

No matter who thought of it, the idea appealed strongly to both men. But before they could begin work, Marco had to write to his father in Venice and ask him to send the notes Marco had made on their journeys. He could not possibly remember all the names and facts he needed without the notes.

The prison authorities seemed to have no objection to any of this. So, before long the notes arrived and Marco and Rustichello got busy.

"Ye emperors, kings, dukes, marquises, earls, and knights, and all other people desirous of knowing the diversities of the races of mankind, as well as the diversities of kingdoms, provinces, and regions of all parts of the East," begins the prologue, "read through this book, and ye will find in it the greatest and most marvelous characteristics of the peoples especially of Armenia, Persia, India, and Tartary, as they are severally related in the present work by Marco Polo, a wise and learned citizen of Venice, who states distinctly what things he saw and what things he heard from others. For this book will be a truthful one." Marco must have dictated the book in Venetian. Later then, Rustichello would translate it into French. Here and there, echoes of the writer's former tales can be heard (such as "Ye emperors, kings, dukes," etc.). But most of it is a clear and simple retelling of what Marco saw and heard.

Meanwhile, battles between the Genoese and their enemies continued and thousands more captives crammed the prisons. Many starved to death. Others died of disease. Marco and Rustichello worked as hard and as quickly as they could. Who knew? They might be the next to die.

They finished the book, *The Travels of Marco Polo*, in 1298. No doubt they heaved a great sigh of relief. But their time in prison had not ended. A peace treaty between Venice and Genoa was not ratified until July of 1299. On August 28, the Venetian prisoners were set free. A treaty between Genoa and Pisa took place at about the same time, so Rustichello must have gone home too.

Marco had been in prison about four years. Rustichello had been there much longer. It was a horrible thing to go through. But if these two had not been forced together that way, the world probably would have never had one of its most fascinating books.

Copies of the French version were made right away. Soon the book was translated into other languages as well. Historians, mapmakers, and other explorers used it often. Christopher Columbus even carried a copy with him in 1492. Parts of the book from a 1460 version turned up hundreds of years later in a walled-up section of a castle in Ireland. They had been translated into Gaelic.

Germany first printed *The Travels of Marco Polo* at Nuremberg in 1477. It was one of the first books ever to be printed in Europe. Since then there have been many editions based on many hand-copied manuscripts. Not all of these are the same. Scholars do not think they have yet found Marco and Rustichello's original manuscript.

That might be an exciting discovery some day. But in the meantime, thousands of people over the centuries have marveled at the lands and people of Kublai Khan's East, thanks to that "wise and learned citizen of Venice," Marco Polo and his fellow prisoner.

Marco Polo's house in Venice

Chapter 13

THE LATER YEARS

Marco must have been exhausted by the time he reached Venice again. Prison life was not easy for anyone, not even for a favored prisoner as he had been. For a while it seemed as if all he wanted was to live quietly. His family bought a mansion in the San Giovanni Chrisostomo section of Venice. To that house Marco at long last brought a wife, Donata Badoer.

He was forty-five when he married, almost old in that day and age. No one knows much about Donata, except that she was the daughter of Vitale Badoer and came with a good dowry. Eventually the couple had three daughters, Fantina, Bellela, and Moreta.

Marco's father, Nicolo, died around the time of the wedding, and Marco saw to it that he had a fine tomb. Ramusio called it "a great sarcophagus of living stone . . . placed under the portico which is before the Church of San Lorenzo of this city, on the right-hand side as one enters . . ."

Then Marco went back to the business of being a merchant. Plenty of goods were passing through Venice. From England came wool and tin in exchange for spices from the East. Baghdad furnished brocade, which also made its way to England, and France as well. People everywhere, but especially in Switzerland, wanted Venetian glass. Civil war in the Italian city of Lucca drove her weavers to Venice, and soon fine silk and velvet goods joined the long list of Venetian merchandise. Marco, of course, was determined to get his share of the profits—and he did.

When the business day ended, he could try to relax at home with his family, although relaxing might have been a bit difficult in the Polo home. In that one house lived Uncle Maffeo and his wife, Marco's half-brother Maffeo and his family, the unmarried half-brother Giovannino, Stefano, his wife, and their five children, and Marco with his own growing family. Such a mixture of relatives in a home was not unusual back then when families were very close. But life at the Polos could not have been too peaceful.

In spite of his successful business and crowded home life, Marco sometimes felt sad. Part of him still longed for the East and the life of adventure he had led there. To comfort himself, he told the tales of his travels again and again. After a while, people grew sick of hearing them. They began to call him Messer Marco Milione (Master Marco of the Millions) because of the huge numbers he used when talking about the wealth of the East. Often they let him know that they did not believe most of what he said. That must have hurt.

In later centuries, scholars and scientists would prove that

Marco had been an amazingly accurate reporter. The few really fantastic things he noted came from stories told him by others, not events seen with his own eyes. He was always careful to state which was which too.

But it would be a long time after his death before many other explorers could reach the East. Gradually Mongol control weakened, and the Chinese drove the invaders out of their lands. Then they slammed shut the gates to foreigners.

During the later part of Marco's life, Venice herself seethed with riots, rebellions, and civil discontent. But such political unrest did not interest the merchant. He kept his eye on his coffers and his trading vessels and let the rebels go their own way.

For a time, he seemed to be quite a rich man. Both his uncle and his half-brother Maffeo died before him and left him much of their property. But not even this could satisfy him. Perhaps he tried too hard to channel the general restlessness and unhappiness he felt into his business. In any case, records show that he went to court several times—even against his own cousin—when he thought he had not gotten his full share in some dealing.

Eventually his daughters grew up. Fantina and Bellela married and he gave each of them a generous dowry. Marco liked his sons-in-law and began working closely with them. Maybe they had not heard his tales so often and were more willing to listen.

By winter of 1323, Marco was seventy years old, a tremendous age for that time. He was growing weaker, though, and nothing the doctors did could help. By January 8, 1324, his family knew that he was dying. According to custom, they sent for a priest so he could make his will.

Marco did not have a huge fortune anymore. Perhaps he had never been as rich as he had seemed. Or perhaps he had lost money in his later years. But he still had enough to provide comfortably for his wife and daughters. He made special provisions for Moreta, who had not married yet. She, he said, should have as much as her sisters received in their dowries, plus the rest of her inheritance. He also left sums to various churches, guilds, and monasteries. Finally, he set free his Tartar slave, Peter, and left him some money.

One legend says that as Marco lay dying, the priest asked him if he wanted to admit at last that some of the tales he had told were not true.

"I did not tell half of what I saw," Marco supposedly replied, "for I knew I would not be believed."

Just before midnight, on January 8, he died. According to his wishes, his family buried him beside his father at the Church of San Lorenzo. Over the centuries, that church has changed so completely that the graves can no longer be found.

Although Moreta Polo eventually married, Fantina was the only one of Marco's daughters to have children. Before long, this branch of the family died out. So today Marco Polo has neither descendents nor a public tomb to keep his memory alive. But he does not need them. The full life he lived and the book describing his adventures make him one of the most remembered people in history.

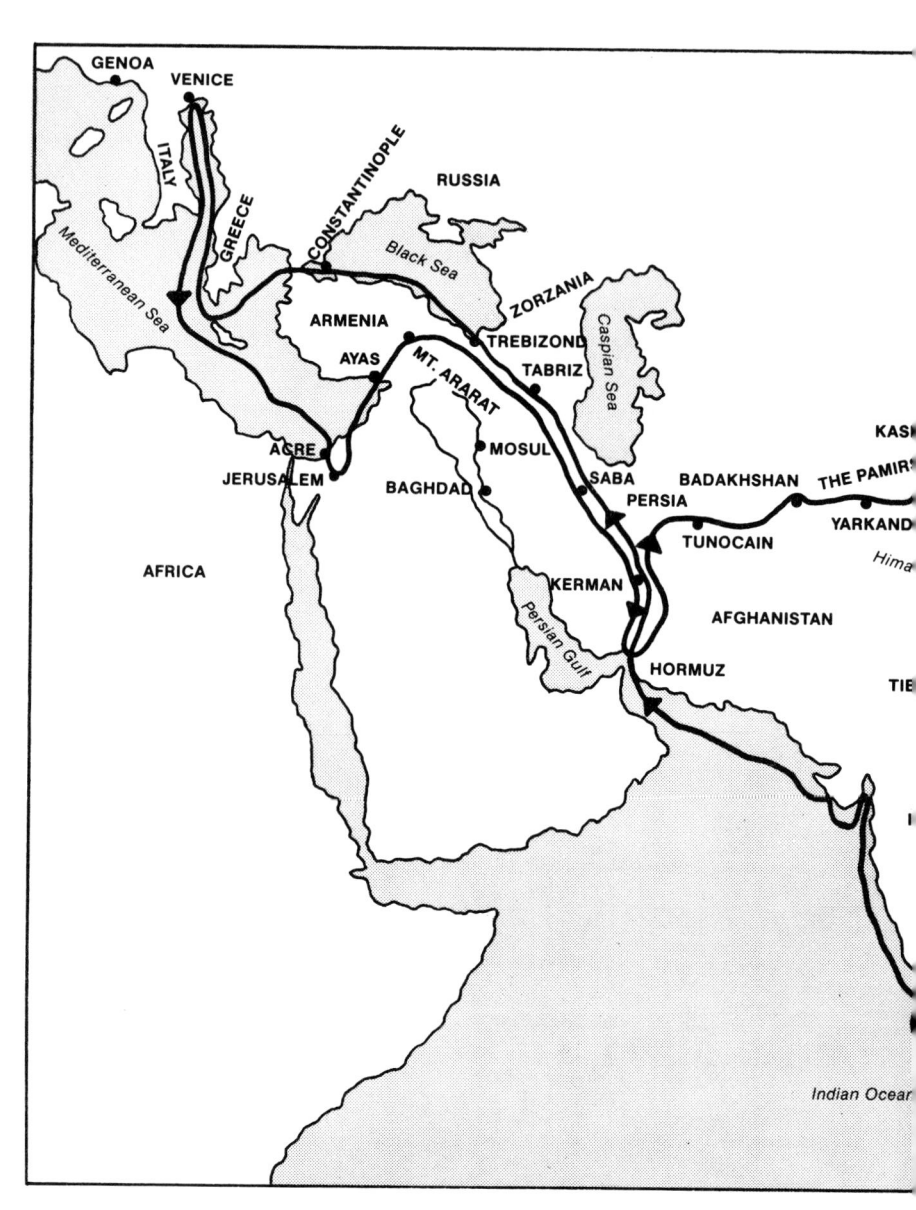

Probable route Marco Polo, his father, and uncle followed in their 24 years of travel.

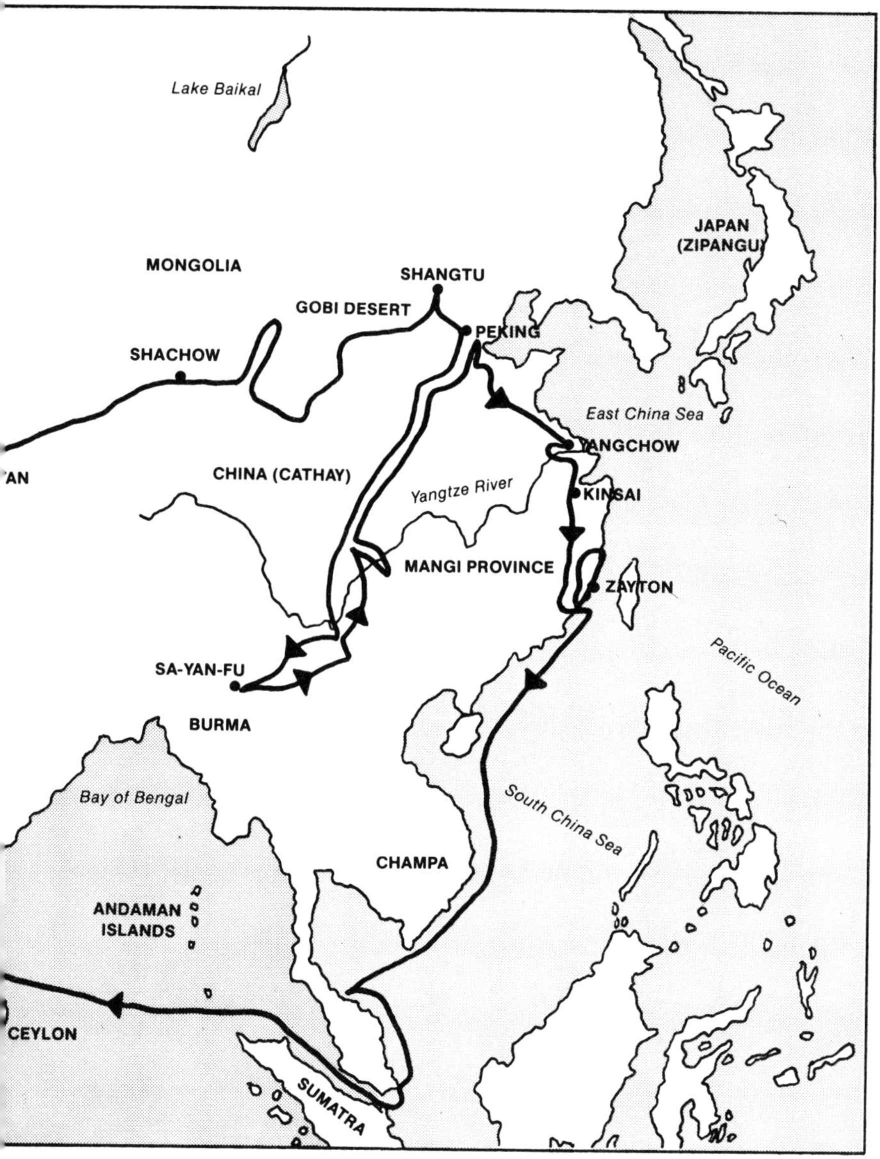

Lake Baikal
MONGOLIA
SHANGTU
GOBI DESERT
PEKING
SHACHOW
JAPAN
(ZIPANGU)
East China Sea
YANGCHOW
AN
CHINA (CATHAY)
Yangtze River
KINSAI
MANGI PROVINCE
ZAYTON
SA-YAN-FU
Pacific Ocean
BURMA
Bay of Bengal
South China Sea
CHAMPA
ANDAMAN
ISLANDS
CEYLON
SUMATRA

Marco Polo 1254-1324

1253 Nicolo and Maffeo Polo begin their first journey to China.
1254 Marco Polo is born.
1256 A grandson of Genghis Khan, Mongol Hulagu, founds dynasty in Persia.
1258 Genoa loses war with Venice. Mongols sack Baghdad.
1260 King Manfred of Sicily rules most of Italy.
1261 Michael VIII Paleologus regains Constantinople for the Holy Roman Empire.
1264 Genoese fleet off the coast of Sicily is defeated by the Venetians. The city of Peking is founded. Kublai Khan becomes ruler of the Mongol Empire.
1265 Dante Alighieri, Italian poet, is born. Clement IV becomes Pope (to 1268).
1266 Giotto (Giotto di Bondone), the Italian painter, architect, and sculptor, is born. King Manfred of Sicily is killed by Charles of Anjou, brother of Louis IX of France.
1268 Charles (Charles I) of Anjou becomes king of Naples and Sicily.
1269 Marco Polo's father, Nicolo, returns from his travels and meets his young son.
1271 Marco Polo sails with his father and uncle for the Mediterranean and Acre. Gregory X becomes pope. Kublai Khan established the Yuan dynasty in China.
1273 Thomas Aquinas, an Italian Dominican monk and philosopher, writes *Summa Theologia*, a basic work of the Roman Catholic church.
1274 Kublai Khan and his Mongols fail to conquer Japan. Thomas Aquinas dies.
1275 Marco Polo enters into the service of Kublai Khan (and remains so until 1292). The Italian astronomer, Mondino di Luzzi, is born.
1276 The year of the four popes: Gregory X, Innocent V, Hadrian V, and John XXI.
1277 The Mongols defeat the Burmese.
1278 The glass mirror is invented. St. Maria Novella in Florence, Italy, is built.
1279 Kublai Khan takes control of southern China.
1281 Typhoon stops Mongol invasion of Japan.
1282 Sicilians revolt against French rule.
1284 Genoa defeats Pisa in Italy, thus beginning Pisa's decline. Sequins are first coined in Venice.
1287 The Mongol Empire begins free travel and trade with Europe. The Mongols invade Burma.
1289 Block printing is practiced in Ravenna, Italy.
1290 Spectacles are invented.
1291 Turks conquer Acre, ending Christian rule in the East.
1292 Marco Polo begins his journey home from China. Dante Alighieri writes *Vita Nuova*, lyric poems.
1294 Kublai Khan dies.
1295 Marco Polo returns to Italy.
1296 Marco Polo is imprisoned in Genoa. The building of the Florence, Italy, Cathedral begins under Arnolfo di Cambio.
1298 *The Travels of Marco Polo* is written.

1299 Marco Polo is released from prison. Venice and Genoa sign a treaty of peace. Mongols invade India.
1302 Dante is exiled from Florence.
1303 Rome University is founded.
1304 Petrarch (Francesco Petrarca), the Italian poet, is born. Mongols defeated by army of the Sultanate of Delhi, India.
1306 Giotto completes frescoes in Santa Maria dell'Arena, Padua.
1307 Dante composes his *Divine Comedy*.
1309 The Doge's Palace in Venice is built on the site of earlier palaces.
1313 The German Grey Friar Berthold Schwartz invents gunpowder.
1314 Giotto paints frescoes in the church of St. Croce, Florence.
1321 Dante dies at Ravenna, Italy.
1323 Thomas Aquinas is canonized.
1324 Marco Polo dies.
1477 *The Travels of Marco Polo* is printed in Germany.

INDEX - *Page numbers in boldface type indicate illustrations.*

Acre, Syria, 21, 23, 24, 25
Adam (biblical), 78
Adriatic Sea, 11, 17, 86
Aegean Sea, 17, 86
Africa, 12
Anatolia, 27
Andaman Islands, 77
animals, descriptions of, 27, 29, 32, 33, 36, 38, **52**, 62, 64, **74**, 76, 77, 79, 80, 82
Apusca (Persian messenger), 71, 72, 73
Arabian Nights, The, 83
Arctic Ocean, 18
Argon (grandnephew of Kublai Khan), 71, 85
Armenia, 21, 25, 26, 91
Arsenal, the (Venice), 14
Arthur, King, and Knights of the Round Table, 91
asbestos, 33
Asia, 21, 31
Asia Minor, 12
Badakhshan, 31
Badoer, Donata (wife of Marco Polo), 95, 98
Badoer, Vitale (father of Donata), 95
Baghdad, 28, 95
Balkh, 31
Balthasar (Wise Man), 29
Bangala, province of, 65
Barka Khan (grandson of Genghis Khan), 18-19
Basman, Sumatra, 76, 77
bathing habits, 15, 20, 56, 66, 80
Black Sea, 86
Bokhara, 19
Bolgana (wife of Argon), 71
Bolgara, 18
Brahman caste, 81-82
Buddha, 78-79
Buddhist lamas, 37
Burma, 64
caliph (of Baghdad), 28-29
canals, 11, 66

cannabis, 31
cannibals, 77
Caspar (Wise Man), 29
Cathay (China), 32
Ceylon, 78-79
Champa (Vietnam), 76
Chin, 44
China, 19, 28, 32, 44, 45, 46, 57, 61, 65, 76, 83, 85, 89, 97; discoveries and inventions in, 55-56
Chinghintalis, 33
Christianity, 20-21, 28-29, 79
Church of San Lorenzo (Venice), 95, 98
Clement IV (pope), 21
coal, 56
Cocachin, Princess, 71, 72, 73, 85, 86
Cogotal (guide), 21
Coja (Persian messenger), 71, 72, 73, 85
Coleridge, Samuel Taylor, 35, 36
Columbus, Christopher, 93
Constantinople, 11, 17, 19, 28, **48**, **49**, 86, 89, 90
crime, 15, 18, 29-30, 31, 58, 62, 86
Crusaders, 21
Curzola (Dalmatian island), 89
Dalmatia, 89
da Vicenza, Fra Nicolo, 26
di Tripoli, Fra Guglielmo, 26
doge of Venice, 13, 14
Dragoian, Sumatra, 77
Egypt, 13
England, 72, 95, 96
English, 35, 36
Europe, 12, 55, 57, 77, 91, 93
Fanfur, Sumatra, 77
Ferlek, Sumatra, 76
foods, 11, 17, 20, 29, 30, 57, 66, 77, 80
France, 96
French language, 90-91, 92, 93
Gaelic language, 93
Garden of Gethsemane, 24
Genghis Khan (grandfather of Kublai

104

Khan), 18, 31, 41, 43, 44-45, 46, 50
Genoa, 89-90, 92
Genoese, 18, 27, 89, 90, 92
Ghazan (son of Argon), 85
Gobi Desert, 32
gondolas, 11, 86
Gouza, 61
Greater Armenia, 27
Greek Islands, 17
Gregory X (pope), 25, 37, **49**
hashish, 31
Hashishin (Assassins), 31
Hindus, 79, 80
Holy City (Jerusalem), 24
Hormuz, Persia, 30, 83
Hulaku (cousin of Barka Khan), 19
Hungary, 18, 45
idol worship, 21, 33, 58-59, 75, 77, 78, 79, 80
Imperial Palace (Peking), 38-39, **52**
India, 12, 18, 30, 71, 79, 82, 91
Indian Ocean, 78
Ireland, 93
Island of Females, 82
Island of Males, 82
Italian, 12
Italian traders, 24
Italy, 12, 57, 90
Japan, 75
Java, 75
Java the Lesser (Sumatra), 76
Jerusalem, 21, 24, 37
Jesus Christ, 13, 21, 24-25, 29, 79
jewels, 13, 14, 29, 31, 32, 66, 78, 79, 81
Joppa, 24
Kaikhatu (brother of Argon), 86
Kain-du, 63
Kanchow, 33
Kangigu, 65
Karaian, 63
Karakorum, 20, 43
Kara-moran River, 61
Karaunas, 29

Karazan, 40, 63
Kashgar, 32
Kerman, Persia, 29, 30
Khanbalik (Peking), 20, 38, 58, 61, 71, 78; capital of Kublai Khan's empire, 38; description of, 38-39; life at court in, 38-40
Khotan, 32
Kinsai (Hangchow), 66-68
Knights of the Round Table, 91
Knights Templars, 26
koumiss, 20, 39-40, 43
kowtow, 36
Kublai Khan, 18, 19, 20-21, 33, 45-46, 78, 93; allows the Polos to return home, 72; becomes khan, 46; conquests by, 46, 62, 65; death of, 85; description of capital, 38-40; description of summer palace, 35-38; failure to conquer Japan, 75; golden tablets of, 20-21, 26, 72; Marco Polo as servant of, 40-41, 46, 61; interest in Christianity by, 20-21, 25, 26; meets Marco Polo, 37; method of rule, 57-59, 76; refuses to let Polos leave, 70-71; second visit of Nicolo and Maffeo Polo with, 36-37; use of Chinese discoveries and systems by, 55-56
Kublai Khan (illustrations), **52, 74**; with Marco Polo, **54**; with Nicolo and Maffeo Polo, **34, 51**
"Kubla Khan: Or, a Vision in a Dream" (poem), 35, 36
Kuyuk (son of Ogadai), 45
Laias (Ayas), Lesser Armenia, 25, 26, 27, 89
Lambri, Sumatra, 77
languages, 11, 12, 35, 40, 86-87, 90, 91, 92, 93
La Sensa (Ascension Day), 13
Lazarus (biblical), 25
legal customs, 81
Lesser Armenia, 27
Lido, 13, 86

105

Lop (Charklik), 32
Lucca, Italy, 96
macaroni, 57
Madagascar, 82-83
mail service (Chinese), 55-56
Malabar, 79, 80, 81
Mangi, China, 65, 75
Mangu (son of Ogadai), 45-46
Martha (biblical), 25
"Master the Apostle" (the pope), 20
Mediterranean, 23, 24, 89
Melchior (Wise Man), 29
Mien, 65
Mongolia, 71
Mongolian plains, 41
Mongols, 18, 20, 41, 57, 58, 97; failure to conquer Japan by, 75; forming the empire of the, 43-46, 62, 64; tribal life of, 41-43; warfare between tribes of, 71
mosaics, 13, 24
Mosul, 28
Mount Ararat, 27
Muslims, 28, 31, 79, 80
muslin, 28
Nestorian Christians, 28
North Africa, 12
Nuremberg, Germany, 93
Ogadai (son of Genghis Khan), 45
oil (petroleum), 27-28
"Old Man of the Mountain," 31
Oucaca, 19
Ovis poli, 32
Pacific Ocean, 18
Palace of the Doges (Venice), **84**
Palazzo del Capitano del Popolo (prison), 90
Pala d'Oro, 13
Pamirs, 32
paper money, 55
Pax Tatarica, 18
Peking, China, 33, 38
Persia, 29, 44, 71, 72, 82, 85, 91
Persian Gulf, 30

Peter (slave of Marco Polo), 87, 98
Piazza San Marco (Saint Mark's Square), 13
Pisa, Italy, 90, 92
Plateau of Iran, 30
Poland, 45
Polo, Bellela (daughter of Marco Polo), 95, 97
Polo, Fantina (daughter of Marco Polo), 95, 97, 98
Polo, Giovannino (half-brother of Marco Polo), 87, 96
Polo, Maffeo (half-brother of Marco Polo), 87, 96, 97
Polo, Maffeo (uncle of Marco Polo), 11, 17, **34**, **49**, **51**, **60**, 96, 97; becomes a magistrate, 88; first trip to the East, 17-22; homecoming in Venice, 86-88; as Kublai Khan's ambassador, 72; second meeting with Kublai Khan, 36-37; second trip back home, 72-73, 76-86; second trip to the East, 23-33; wife of, 11, 87; wishes to return to Venice, second time, 69-71
Polo, Marco: birth of, 11; childhood of, 12-16; children of, 95, 96, 97, 98; death of, 98; descriptions of animals by, 62, 63, 64, 65, 76, 77, 82-83; descriptions of Chinese inventions by, 55-56; dictating his story to Rustichello, 91-92; disbelief of his stories, 77, 96, 98; education of, 12-16, 40; first meeting of with his father, 22; life in prison, 90-92; life with the Khan, 37-41; marriage of, 95; merchant life of, 88-89, 95-96, 97; mother of, 11, 12, 22; observations on Burmese life by, 64; observations of Chinese life by, 61-62, 65-68; observations on Mongol life by, 55-59; observations on Tibet by, 62-64; religious beliefs of, 13; servant of Kublai Khan, 40-41, 61, 65, 72; sheep named after him, 32; sickness of, 31; step-mother of, 23; tales of Japan by, 75; traveling to the East, 23-33; *Travels of Marco Polo, The*, 92-93, 99; trip

back to Venice, 72-73, 76-86; untrue legends about, 56-57, 82; voyage to India, 71; wishes to return to Venice, 69-71; writings as inspiration to other writers, 35-36
Polo, Marco (illustrations), 4, 53, 60; house in Venice of, 94; with Kublai Khan, 54
Polo, Moreta (daughter of Marco Polo), 95, 98
Polo, Nicolo (father of Marco Polo), 11, 17, 34, 49, 51, 60, 91; death of, 95; first trip to the East, 17-22; homecoming in Venice, 86-88; other children named, 87; named as Kublai Khan's ambassador, 72; second marriage, 23, 87; second meeting with Kublai Khan, 36-37; second trip back to Venice, 72-73, 76-86; second trip to the East, 23-33; wishes to return to Venice, second time, 69-71
Polo, Stefano (half-brother of Marco Polo), 87, 96
pope, 20, 21, 23, 25, 72
punishment for crimes, 15
Purchas, Samuel, 35
Queen of the Adriatic (Venice), 12
Ramusio (historian), 90, 95
Russia, 12, 45
Rustichello (writer), 90-93
Saba, Persia, 29
safe-conduct tablets, 20-21, 26, 72, 86
Saint Anthony of Padua (monastery in Venice), 15
Saint Mark, 11, 13, 90
Saint Mark's Church (Venice), 13, 15, 24, 84, 86
Sakyamuni (Buddha), 78-79
Samara, Sumatra, 77
San Giovanni Chrisostomo (Venice), 94, 95
Sapurgan, 31
Saracens, 26
Sa-yan-fu, China, 65
Sea of Marmora, 17

Shachow (Tunhuang), 33
Shangtu, China, 20, 33, 35-36, 37-38
shipbuilding, 14, 30, 66
sickness, 30, 31, 32, 63
silk, 61, 62
slavery, 12, 30
slaves, 12, 18, 87
Sogomonbarchan (Sakyamuni), 78
Solomon's Temple, 24
"Son of Heaven" (Emperor of China), 46
South China Sea, 72
Spain, 72
spices, 12, 66, 76, 95
Sudan, in the Crimea, 18
sultan of Persia, 44
Sumatra, 76-77
suttee, 80
Switzerland, 96
Tabriz, 29, 85, 86
Tangut, 33
Tartars, 12, 45
Tartary, 91
Temuchin (Genghis Khan), 41, 43
Teobaldo of Piacenza, 21, 24, 25; becomes pope Gregory X, 25
Tibet, 37, 62-64
Tiepolo, Lorenzo (doge of Venice), 14
trade, 11, 18, 19, 24, 44, 66, 76, 77, 89, 95
transportation, 11, 13, 18, 19, 25, 27, 30, 42, 55-56, 64, 66, 72, 75
travel, 11, 17; dangers of, 18, 19, 24, 26, 29-30, 32, 62, 63, 71, 77, 85, 87
Travels of Marco Polo, The, 92-93, 99; dictated in Venetian, 92; printed in Germany, 93; translated into French, 92-93; translated into Gaelic, 93
Trebizond, 86
Tunocain, 31
Turkey, 12, 27
Turkomania (Anatolia), 27
turquoise, 29
Uladai (Persian messenger), 71, 72, 73

unicorn, 76
Venetian: glass, 96; language, 92; people, 18, 27, 56, 89, 90
Venice, Italy, 10, 11, 12, 18, 19, 21, 23, 38, 45, 47, 72, 84, 86, 88, 89, 91, 92, 94, 95, 96, 97; doge of, 13, 14; everyday life in, 14-16; religion in, 13
Vietnam, 76
Western church, 20
Wise Men (three), 29
Xanadu (Shangtu), 35
yaks, 33
Yangchow, China, 65
Yangtze River, 66
Yarkand, 32
Yesukai (father of Genghis Khan), 41, 43
yogi caste, 81-82
Yunnan, China (province), 61
yurts, 42, 43
Zayton, China (port), 72
Zipangu (Japan), 75
Zorzania, 27

ABOUT THE AUTHOR

Carol Greene has degrees in English literature and musicology. She has worked in international exchange programs, as an editor, and as a teacher. She now lives in St. Louis, Missouri, and writes full-time. She has had over fifty books published—most of them for children. Other Childrens Press biographies by Ms. Greene include *Louisa May Alcott, Hans Christian Andersen, Marie Curie,* and *Thomas Alva Edison* in the People of Distinction series and *Sandra Day O'Connor, Mother Teresa, Indira Nehru Gandhi,* and *Diana, Princess of Wales* in the Picture Story Biography series.